LEARNERS FOR LIFE

STUDENT APPROACHES TO LEARNING

RESULTS FROM PISA 2000

Cordula Artelt
Jürgen Baumert
Nele Julius-McElvany
Jules Peschar

OECD
ORGANISATION FOR ECONOMIC CO-OPERATION AND DEVELOPMENT

ORGANISATION FOR ECONOMIC CO-OPERATION AND DEVELOPMENT

Pursuant to Article 1 of the Convention signed in Paris on 14th December 1960, and which came into force on 30th September 1961, the Organisation for Economic Co-operation and Development (OECD) shall promote policies designed:

- to achieve the highest sustainable economic growth and employment and a rising standard of living in member countries, while maintaining financial stability, and thus to contribute to the development of the world economy;

- to contribute to sound economic expansion in member as well as non-member countries in the process of economic development; and

- to contribute to the expansion of world trade on a multilateral, non-discriminatory basis in accordance with international obligations.

The original member countries of the OECD are Austria, Belgium, Canada, Denmark, France, Germany, Greece, Iceland, Ireland, Italy, Luxembourg, the Netherlands, Norway, Portugal, Spain, Sweden, Switzerland, Turkey, the United Kingdom and the United States. The following countries became members subsequently through accession at the dates indicated hereafter: Japan (28th April 1964), Finland (28th January 1969), Australia (7th June 1971), New Zealand (29th May 1973), Mexico (18th May 1994), the Czech Republic (21st December 1995), Hungary (7th May 1996), Poland (22nd November 1996), Korea (12th December 1996) and the Slovak Republic (14th December 2000). The Commission of the European Communities takes part in the work of the OECD (Article 13 of the OECD Convention).

FOREWORD

What are students like as learners as they approach the end of compulsory education? The answer matters greatly, not only because those with stronger approaches to learning get better results at school but also because young adults able to set learning goals and manage their own learning are much more likely to take up further study and become lifelong learners.

The OECD Programme for International Student Assessment (PISA) provides a unique opportunity to look at how students approach learning, alongside how well they perform in key subject areas. This report analyses the results, focusing on aspects of students' motivation, self-belief and use of various learning strategies that together make it more likely that a student will become a confident and self-regulated learner.

The results confirm strong links between such student approaches to learning and measurable student outcomes. For example, students showing strong interest in reading and those who are more confident of their ability to solve problems that they find difficult are more likely to perform well. The report also shows particularly strong links between students' tendency to control their own learning, by consciously monitoring progress towards personal goals, and their motivation and self-belief. This suggests that effective learning cannot simply be taught as a skill but also depends heavily on developing positive attitudes.

This report offers policy-makers a fine-grained analysis of which particular learner characteristics are prevalent in different countries. It also identifies differences between the approaches to learning of various groups, including male and female students, and those from more and less advantaged social backgrounds. The results point to ways in which education systems can focus efforts to help different groups of students become more effective learners.

PISA is a collaborative effort, bringing together scientific expertise from the participating countries, steered jointly by their governments on the basis of shared, policy-driven interests. Participating countries take responsibility for the project at the policy level through a Board of Participating Countries. Experts from participating countries serve on working groups that are charged with linking the PISA policy objectives with the best available substantive and technical expertise in the field of international comparative assessment of educational outcomes. Through participating in these expert groups, countries ensure that the PISA assessment instruments are internationally valid and take into account the cultural and curricular contexts of OECD Member countries, that they provide a realistic basis for measurement, and that they place an emphasis on authenticity and educational validity. The frameworks and assessment instruments for PISA 2000 are the product of a multi-year development process and were adopted by OECD Member countries in December 1999.

This report is the product of a concerted effort between the authors Cordula Artelt, Jürgen Baumert, Nele Julius-McElvany and Jules Peschar, the countries participating in PISA, the experts and institutions working within the framework of the PISA Consortium, and the OECD. The report was prepared by the OECD Directorate for Education under the direction of Kooghyang Ro and Andreas Schleicher. The development of the report was steered by the Board of Participating Countries, chaired by Eugene Owen of the National Center for Education Statistics in the United States. Annex E of the report lists the members of the various PISA bodies as well as the individual experts and consultants who have contributed to this report and to PISA in general.

The report is published on the responsibility of the Secretary-General of the OECD.

TABLE OF CONTENTS

THE PISA SURVEY AND STUDENT APPROACHES TO LEARNING

Introductory overview: Approaches to learning and why they are important

Education systems aim to enable students not just to acquire knowledge but also to become capable, confident and enthusiastic learners. At school, students who have positive approaches to learning, in terms of both attitudes and behaviours, tend to enjoy good learning outcomes. Beyond school, children and adults who have developed the ability and motivation to learn on their own initiative are well-placed to become lifelong learners. Thus, an overall assessment of the outcomes of schooling needs to consider not only students' knowledge and understanding but also their approaches to learning.

The Programme for International Student Assessment (PISA) aims to measure such wider outcomes of schooling, at the same time as assessing student performance in terms of reading, mathematical and scientific literacies. Key results from the PISA 2000 survey have been presented elsewhere[1]. This report focuses on the results in terms of approaches to learning, looking at the learning strategies that students adopt, at their motivation and at their confidence in their own learning abilities. The survey's investigation of the learning approaches of 15-year-olds in 26 countries, set alongside its assessment of their knowledge and skills, creates a unique resource. It makes it possible: to understand better how various aspects of student attitudes to learning and their learning behaviour relate to each other and to learning outcomes; to observe how these relationships differ across countries; and to note the distribution of relevant characteristics among different students, across and within countries.

These findings build on existing knowledge about approaches to learning. Prior research has identified some key features of these approaches that frame the analysis of PISA results. It shows that learning is more likely to be effective where a student plays a proactive role in the learning process – for example drawing on strong motivation and clear goals to select an appropriate learning strategy. Such a proactive process is often described as "self-regulated" learning.

A large-scale survey cannot easily make a direct assessment of the extent to which students actually regulate their learning in practice. However, research has also identified some measurable characteristics of students that are associated with the tendency to regulate one's own learning, as well as with better student performance. These characteristics are the three main aspects of approaches to learning that students were asked about in PISA: their confidence in their own learning abilities (self-related beliefs), their motivation and their tendency to adopt certain learning strategies.

The analysis that follows does not, therefore, take a neutral view of alternative learning approaches, but rather centres on some positive features that put students in a better position to regulate their own learning. However, this does not mean that it prescribes a single, uniform learning approach – the evidence shows for example that different kinds of strategy can contribute to positive learning outcomes. Moreover, the analysis also considers a further dimension of student approaches concerning alternative styles of learning not associated directly with self-regulation, *i.e.,* whether students feel positive about learning in co-operative or in competitive situations.

The remainder of this chapter sets out the context for the presentation of PISA results that follows. First, it explains how the measurement of approaches to learning fits into the PISA survey. Next, it summarises existing evidence on this subject and how that affects the way in which the PISA survey tackles the issue. The chapter then sets out specifically what students were asked in PISA about how they approach learning and how this relates to various aspects found to be important by prior research. Lastly, the chapter concludes by summarising what PISA can and what it cannot, add to existing knowledge about student approaches to learning.

The PISA survey, and where approaches to learning fit in

In response to the need for internationally comparable evidence on student performance, the OECD launched the Programme for International Student Assessment in 1997, carrying out the first triennial survey in 2000. Nationally representative samples of 15-year-old students in 32 countries undertook an assessment and completed a questionnaire about themselves, with principals also completing a questionnaire about their schools.

This effort emerged from and is guided by the OECD's programme on Indicators of Education Systems (INES). The demand for better student outcome indicators applies not just to knowledge and skills, but also to wider outcomes of schooling. A group in INES therefore explored the ways to measure competencies that cut across areas of the school curriculum, whether personal attributes such as active citizenship and generic skills such as problem-solving or learning skills such as the capacity to control one's own learning.

Following a feasibility study (OECD, 1997), the development of PISA is pursuing the objective of measuring wider learning outcomes in a number of ways[2]. In the 2000 survey, the most direct instrument for such measurement was an extra questionnaire, filled out by students in 26 countries, listed in Annex A, about their approaches to learning (this questionnaire sought overall to measure capacity for self-regulated learning). The results of the questionnaire, set alongside the other information gained from PISA on student performance and students' personal characteristics, are the basis of the analysis that follows. The combination of these three types of information – student approaches to learning, student performance and student background – on an internationally comparable basis provides an unprecedented opportunity to explore students' learning capacity across and within countries.

Box A. Participation in the self-regulated learning questionnaire of PISA 2000

---

120 740 students in:

- Twenty-two OECD countries - Australia, Austria, Belgium (Fl.)[3], the Czech Republic, Denmark, Finland, Germany, Hungary, Ireland, Iceland, Italy, Korea, Luxembourg, Mexico, the Netherlands[4], New Zealand, Norway, Portugal, Sweden, Switzerland, Scotland[5] and the United States.

- Four non-OECD countries - Brazil, Latvia, Liechtenstein and the Russian Federation.

The PISA sampling procedure allows the findings to be generalized to the population of 15-year-olds in each participating country.

Existing evidence on approaches to learning, and how this frames PISA's approach

PISA provides an opportunity to explore the extent to which school systems help students acquire learning competencies and dispositions that are essential both for academic success and for learning in later life, allowing job-related development in adulthood and supporting lifelong learning more generally. These learner characteristics can be seen partly as factors that contribute to different levels of performance in school, but also as outcomes of schooling in their own right. The emphasis on students' ability to regulate their own learning is particularly important in carrying learning skills through to less closely directed learning environments beyond the school classroom.

Existing research evidence is important for the construction and interpretation of the survey, both in terms of establishing which aspects of students' learning approaches are important and in terms of developing accurate measures of those approaches.

Understanding effective learning approaches

Research on effective student approaches to learning has focused on understanding what it is for a student to regulate his or her own learning. This focus derives partly from direct evidence (see Box B) that such regulation yields benefits in terms of improved student performance and partly from the assumption, albeit not presently backed by strong research, that lifelong learning relies crucially on self-regulation. The latter view is increasingly important in analysis of educational outcomes. For example a large conceptual study on Defining and Selecting Competencies, carried out by the Swiss Federal Statistical Office and supported by the OECD and the US Department of Education, identified three key categories of the broader outcomes of schooling. One of these, personal skills, was defined in terms of "the ability to act autonomously"[6] (Rychen and Salganik, 2002).

Box B. Students who regulate their learning perform better

There is a broad literature on the effects of self-regulated learning on scholastic achievement. Students who are able to regulate their learning effectively are more likely to achieve specific learning goals. Empirical evidence for such positive effects of regulating one's learning and using learning strategies stems from:

- experimental research (*e.g.*, Willoughby and Wood, 1994);

- research on training (*e.g.*, Lehtinen, 1992; Rosenshine and Meister, 1994); and

- systematic observation of students while they are learning (*e.g.*, Artelt, 2000) including studies that ask students to think aloud about their own awareness of and regulation of learning processes (*e.g.*, Veenman and van Hout-Wolters, 2002).

Studies investigating how students *actually* regulate learning and use appropriate strategies have found particularly strong associations between approaches to learning and performance. Less direct but easier to measure student attitudes and behaviours associated with self-regulated learning, such as their motivation and *tendency* to use certain strategies, are also associated with performance, albeit generally less strongly.

Although there have been varying definitions of self-regulated learning, it is generally understood to involve students in:

- selecting appropriate *learning goals* which guide the learning process;

- using appropriate *knowledge and skills* to direct learning;

- consciously selecting appropriate *learning strategies* appropriate to the task at hand; and

- being *motivated* to learn.

The research (particularly Boekarts, 1999; Zimmerman and Schunk, 2001) demonstrates the importance of a combination of such factors in a particular learning episode. Students must be able to draw simultaneously on a range of resources. Some of these resources are concerned with knowledge about how to process information (cognitive resources) and awareness of different available learning strategies (metacognitive resources). Sometimes self-regulation is more or less equated with the metacognitive ability to take control of the learning process (Winne, 2001; Corno, 1989). However, Boekaerts (1999) has argued that this neglects the equally essential elements linked to learner attitudes and dispositions. Learners may be aware of appropriate learning strategies, but not put them into use (Flavell and Wellman, 1977). This requires in addition motivational resources that contribute to the readiness, for example, to define one's own goals, interpret success and failure appropriately and translate wishes into intentions and plans (Weinert, 1994).

Thus self-regulated learning depends on the interaction between what students know and can do on the one hand and on their motivation and inclinations on the other. PISA's investigation of student approaches to learning is based on a model combining these two broad elements. They interact strongly with each other. For example, students' motivation to learn has a profound impact on their choice of learning strategies because, as discussed below, some strategies require a considerable degree of time and effort to implement (Hatano, 1998).

Measuring whether students are likely to adopt effective approaches to learning

To measure directly whether students adopt certain approaches to learning, one would need to examine their actions in specific situations. This requires in-depth interview methods of a type that is not possible in a large-scale survey like PISA (Artelt, 2000; Boekaerts, 1999; Lehtinen, 1992). On the other hand, such a survey is able to measure certain *characteristics* of students, associated with particular learning approaches. Specifically, it can measure prerequisites to self-regulated learning: necessary preconditions that do not guarantee that a student will regulate his or her learning on specific occasions (which also requires a capacity for adaptive behaviour), but are associated with a tendency to do so. These are in the three categories mentioned in Figure 1.1 – motivation, self-concept and tendency to use certain learning strategies. By looking at such characteristics individually, one can get a good indication of whether a student is likely to regulate his or her own learning. This is the approach taken by PISA.

At the centre of this approach is the hypothesis that students who approach learning with confidence, with strong motivation and with a range of learning strategies at their disposal are more likely to be successful learners, because they take responsibility for and regulate their learning. This hypothesis has been borne out by the research referred to in Box B.

PISA 2000 used a questionnaire to ask students about these characteristics. To what extent can one expect accurate self-assessment by 15-year-olds of their learning approaches? The evidence shows that by the age of 15, students' knowledge about their own learning and their ability to give valid answers to questionnaire items have developed considerably (Schneider, 1996). It can thus be assumed that we gain a realistic picture of students' learning approaches from this method.

The PISA questionnaire on student approaches to learning, and what student characteristics it identifies

Following the principle, described above, that certain characteristics make it more likely that students will approach learning in beneficial ways, the PISA survey identified 11 such characteristics[7] and asked students several questions about each of them. These categories came under the three broad elements of motivation, self-related beliefs and learning strategies. In addition, it asked students about two other aspects of their approach to learning: whether they have preferences, respectively, for co-operative or competitive learning. These do not directly relate to students' regulation of their own learning. Thus there were 13 categories in all and for each, student responses were used to score them on a scale rating the degree to which they have the relevant characteristics.

Figure 1.1 sets out the 13 characteristics being investigated, giving the rationale for their selection, based on previous research, as well as examples of exactly what students were asked. The full set of questions is shown in Annex A.

Note on terminology

This report bases its analysis on the individual *characteristics* of students as learners (or learner characteristics) and describes them collectively as *approaches to learning* (or learning approaches). Students are said to be more likely to *regulate their learning* to the extent that they have characteristics in the three categories listed in Figure 1.1 — student strategies, motivational preferences and self-related beliefs, but having these characteristics is not direct evidence that such regulation is taking place. Self-related beliefs are sometimes referred to in terms of *self-confidence*, indicating that such beliefs are positive.

In summarising student responses to these questions, the analysis below assigns each student a score for each of the 13 characteristics, indicating the strength of each learning attribute. In each case, this is measured on a scale constructed from the replies to three to five questions related to that characteristic. Each scale was constructed by giving students a score from 1 to 4 for different responses (higher numbers representing more positive responses) and taking a mean score for all the questions. For example, when asked about aspects of memorising material, a student might report two statements being true "sometimes" and two being true "often" — the middle two of the four frequency categories. This would result in a mean score of 2.5, which would be that student's score for memorisation. In the case of questions requiring agreement or disagreement, 2.5 represents a point of "neutrality", since responses 1 and 2 are negative (disagreement) and 3 and 4 are positive (agreement). In these cases students with above 2.5 can be said to have positive learning characteristics and those with below to have negative characteristics. For example, students with below 2.5 on the reading interest scale show overall a lack of interest in reading; those with below 2.5 on the three self-concept scales have a negative self-concept, *i.e.,* lack confidence in their ability to master particular school tasks.[8]

What PISA adds to knowledge in this field, and what it does not

By measuring student approaches to learning alongside performance in a large and representative international survey, PISA adds to the existing knowledge in several important respects.

First, the survey allows specific research findings on relationships between student attitudes, behaviours and performance to be generalised across countries and for the strength of these relationships to be compared across countries. It can tell us, for example, the extent to which an association between interest

Figure 1.1

13 characteristics of students as learners, measured by PISA

Category of characteristics and rationale	Student characteristics used to construct a scale to report results	Example of statement shown to students	What students were required to do
A. Student strategies Learning strategies are the plans students select to achieve their goals: the ability to do so distinguishes competent learners who can regulate their learning (Zimmerman and Martinez-Pons, 1990; Brown *et al*, 1983). Cognitive strategies that require information processing skills include memorisation and elaboration, shown here, as well as others such as the ability to transfer information from one medium to another. Metacognitive strategies, implying conscious regulation of learning, are summed up in the concept of control strategies.	1. Uses *memorisation* strategies. These involve verbatim representations of knowledge stored in memory with little or no further processing.	"When I study, I memorise as much as possible."	State frequency*
	2. Uses *elaboration* strategies to connect new material to prior learning. By exploring how knowledge learned in other contexts relates to new material, students acquire greater understanding than through simple memorisation.	"When I study, I figure out how material fits in with what I have learned."	State frequency*
	3. Uses *control* strategies to ensure one's learning goals are reached. These strategies involve checking what one has learned and working out what one still needs to learn, allowing learners to adapt their learning to the task at hand. Such strategies are at the heart of the approaches to learning measured by PISA.	"When I study I force myself to check to see if I remember what I have learned."	State frequency*
B. Motivational preferences and volition Motivation can be regarded as the driving force behind learning. One can distinguish motives deriving from *external* rewards for good performance such as praise or future prospects, from *internally* generated motives such as interest in subject areas (Deci and Ryan, 1985; Schiefele, Krapp and Winteler, 1992). Distinct from motivation is volition, shown at the time that learning takes place and leading to effort and persistence (O'Neil and Herl, 1998).	4. Has *instrumental motivation* – *i.e.* a student is encouraged to learn by external rewards such as good job prospects. Longitudinal studies (*e.g.*, Wigfield, Eccles and Rodriguez, 1998) show that such motivation influences both study choices and performance.	"I study to get a job."	State frequency*
	5. Shows *interest in reading* (*See explanation under 6 below*).	"When I read, I sometimes get totally absorbed."	State agreement**
	6. Shows *interest in mathematics* Interest in a subject is a relatively stable orientation affecting intensity and continuity of engagement in learning situations, selection of strategies and depth of understanding. The degree to which students show interest can be seen as an important strength or weakness of school systems.	"Because doing math is fun, I wouldn't want to give it up."	State agreement**
	7. Shows *effort and persistence* – this requires volition – a will to learn shown immediately before and during the learning process.	"When studying, I put forth my best effort."	State frequency*

* Students asked whether statement is true "almost never", "sometimes", "often" or "almost always".

** Students asked whether they "disagree", "disagree somewhat", "agree somewhat" or "agree" with the statement.

Figure 1.1 (continued)

13 characteristics of students as learners, measured by PISA

C. Self-related beliefs Learners form views about their own competence and learning characteristics. These views have been shown to have considerable impact on the way they set goals, the strategies they use and their achievement (Zimmerman, 1999). Two ways of defining these beliefs are in terms of how well students think that they can handle even difficult tasks – *self-efficacy* (Bandura, 1994); and in terms of their belief in their own abilities – *self-concept* (Marsh, 1993). PISA considers both of these. In both cases, confidence in oneself has important benefits for motivation and for the way in which students approach learning tasks.	8. *Self-efficacy* – *i.e.*, believes in own ability to handle learning situations effectively, overcoming difficulties. This affects students' willingness to take on challenging tasks and to make an effort and persist in tackling them: it thus has a key impact on motivation (Bandura, 1994).	"I'm certain I can understand the most difficult material presented in readings."	State frequency*
	9. *Self-concept in reading* – *i.e.*, believes in own verbal competence (*see explanation under 11 below*)	"I learn things quickly in English class."	State agreement**
	10. *Mathematical self-concept* – *i.e.*, believes in own mathematical competence (*see explanation under 11 below*)	"I have always done well in mathematics."	State agreement**
	11. *Academic self-concept* – *i.e.*, believes in own competence in school subjects overall. Belief in one's own abilities is highly relevant to successful learning (Marsh, 1986), as well as being a goal in its own right, affecting well-being and personality development which is especially important to students from less advantaged backgrounds. What students think of their ability in particular subjects is important, not least because research (confirmed in PISA) shows that students who are confident in verbal abilities are not as likely to be confident in mathematical abilities (or vice versa) as the strong correlation between performance in these two domains would suggest. Overall academic confidence is not just the sum of confidence in individual subjects but affected by many factors including the social environment.	"I learn things quickly in most school subjects."	State agreement**
D. Learning situations – preferences A good learner needs to be able to learn both independently and in a group (Baumert, Feld, O'Neil and Peschar, 1998), all the more so in the context of lifelong learning. PISA looked at student preferences for these two learning situations. While no one type of preference is superior, and preference for the two types are not mutually exclusive, this information can give some indication of the approach students will take to co-operative projects in working life.	12. Has preference for *co-operative learning*.	"I learn the most when I work with other students."	State agreement**
	13. Has preference for *competitive learning*.	"Trying to be better than others makes me work well."	State agreement**

* Students asked whether statement is true "almost never", "sometimes", "often" or "almost always".

** Students asked whether they "disagree", "disagree somewhat", "agree somewhat" or "agree" with the statement.

and performance in mathematics, observed by researchers say in the United States, is also observable in Japan. Associations among different motivational, behavioural and performance measures can also give clues to help to build up a better picture of how students come to be effective learners. It is important to note that they cannot directly show that one factor leads to another: for example, observing that well motivated students perform well does not in itself distinguish the extent that performance boosts motivation rather than motivation boosting performance. However, in light of prior research showing, in this case, the central importance of motivation in developing effective learning habits, PISA can build on existing knowledge to estimate the strength of effects already known to exist.

The relationships among different aspects of student approaches to learning and their relationship with performance are analysed in Chapter 2.

Second, PISA allows some comparison of student approaches to learning across countries. To what extent can we compare the degree to which students in different countries have characteristics that help them to be better learners? This issue needs to be approached with caution, since the survey asks students in different countries to make subjective assessments about things such as how hard they work. It cannot be taken for granted that, say, a Korean student who says that she works hard has characteristics comparable to an Australian student who says the same: cultural factors can influence profoundly the way in which such responses are given.

Chapter 3 addresses this issue of comparability across countries and comes to two important conclusions. One is that such differences make it impossible to make valid comparisons of average scores across countries for some of the 13 characteristics, but for others, such comparisons can be meaningful. The other is that even where these averages cannot be compared, it is legitimate to compare the distribution of a particular characteristic among students in different countries. Thus for example while the average effort and persistence claimed by Australian and Korean students may not show the real difference in their effort and persistence, the way in which student scores on this scale are distributed around each country's average can be legitimately compared, in building up country profiles of approaches to learning. Chapter 3 thus analyses differences in approaches to learning across countries and constructs profiles of each country in this respect.

Finally, the relatively large sample sizes in the PISA survey make it possible to look at the characteristics of various subgroups of the student population in terms of their approaches to learning. The analysis of these results, in Chapter 4, helps identify the degree to which weaker approaches to learning are concentrated in certain groups and therefore whether and where remedial help needs to be focused.

The implications of these findings for policy are brought together in Chapter 5.

Notes

1. In particular in *Knowledge and Skills for Life* (OECD, 2001). The results for reading were looked at in closer detail in *Reading for Change* (OECD, 2002b) and various other thematic reports under development are analysing other PISA findings.

2. PISA continues to collect information on broader learning outcomes of 15-year-olds. In addition to the self-regulated learning skills that have been included since PISA 2000, problem solving skill is assessed in PISA 2003.

3. Only the Flemish part of Belgium participated in this part of the survey.

4. The results for the Netherlands are reported, although the response rate in the Netherlands was too low to ensure comparability (see OECD, 2001).

5. In the United Kingdom, only Scotland participated in this part of the survey.

6. The other two were: practical skills, defined in terms of interactive use of tools in the widest possible sense; and social skills, defined in terms of successful participation in socially heterogeneous groups.

7. These 11 student characteristics are a selection of characteristics described in the original PISA framework of self-regulated learning as a "cross-curricular competence". After analysis of field trial data these 11 characteristics were shown not only to be important by theory and research as central components of such learning, but also to be feasible to measure on a internationally comparable basis.

8. Note that this scaling method is not the same as the one used in *Knowledge and Skills for Life* (OECD, 2001), which was based on a "WARM" index centred around the mean OECD score as zero with OECD standard deviation as 1 for each scale. The advantage of the present method is that it allows scores to be related to responses and for positive and negative characteristics to be distinguished on some scales. The overall pattern of results using the two methods is almost identical, since they are highly correlated (r=0.99).

READERS' GUIDE

Data underlying the figures

The data referred to in Chapters 2 to 4 of this report are presented in Annex C.

Calculation of international averages

There are three kinds of international averages:

The *OECD average*, sometimes also referred to as the country average, is the mean of the data values for all OECD countries for which data are available or can be estimated. The OECD average can be used to see how a country compares on a given indicator with a typical OECD country. The OECD average does not take into account the absolute size of the student population in each country, *i.e.*, each country contributes equally to the average.

The *OECD total*, sometimes also referred to as the total average, takes the OECD countries as a single entity, to which each country contributes in proportion to the number of 15-year-olds enrolled in its schools. It illustrates how a country compares with the OECD area as a whole.

Readers should, therefore, keep in mind that the terms *OECD average* and *OECD total* refer to the OECD countries included in the respective comparisons.

The *Total average* is the mean of the data values for all the countries including non-Member countries for which data are available or can be estimated. The total average can be used to see how a country compares on a given indicator with a typical country that participated in the PISA 2000 survey.

The Netherlands are excluded from the estimation of these three averages because low response rates preclude reliable estimates of mean scores. In the case of other countries, data may not be available for specific indicators, or specific categories may not apply.

Index of central tendency

In order to give an overview of the average trend observed among countries, the average of the OECD countries is reported. In some cases, the OECD average is not reported because an average of within-country relationships does not provide meaningful information about relationships across all countries.

Reporting of student data

The report usually uses 15-year-olds as shorthand for the PISA target population. In practice, this refers to students who were aged between 15 years and 3 (complete) months and 16 years and 2 (complete) months at the beginning of the assessment period and who were enrolled in an educational institution, regardless of the grade level or type of institution and of whether they are full-time or part-time students.

Reporting of school data

The principals of the schools in which students were assessed provided information on their schools' characteristics by completing a school questionnaire. Where responses from school principals are presented in this publication, they are weighted so that they are proportionate to the number of 15-year-olds enrolled in the school.

Rounding of figures

Because of rounding, some figures in tables may not exactly add up to the totals. Totals, differences and averages are always calculated on the basis of exact numbers and are rounded only after calculation.

Abbreviations used in this report

The following abbreviations are used in this report:

S.D. Standard deviation

S.E. Standard error

Further documentation

For further information on the PISA assessment instruments and the methods used in PISA, see the *Knowledge and Skills for Life: First Results from PISA 2000* (OECD, 2001), *PISA 2000 Technical Report* (OECD, 2002a) and the PISA Web site (*www.pisa.oecd.org*).

MOTIVATION, SELF–RELATED BELIEFS, LEARNING STRATEGIES AND PERFORMANCE: HOW THEY ARE ASSOCIATED IN PISA

KEY POINTS

- Students in PISA 2000 who reported the greatest strengths in aspects of motivation, self-related beliefs and learning strategies show considerably higher reading literacy performance, on average, than those who are weakest in these respects. Typically, the quarter of students strongest in a particular characteristic perform on average between one-half and one and a half proficiency levels higher than the weakest quarter on the same characteristic, within each country.

- The advantage of having a stronger approach to learning is not always linear: the performance difference between weak and average attributes is not necessarily the same as between average and strong. For example, in the case of controlling one's learning, the group who stands out most from the rest is the quarter of students who make almost no use of such strategies, compared to others who make at least some use. On the other hand, interest in reading is associated with greatest performance differences when comparing the keenest quarter of readers with the rest.

- Relationships between different aspects of how students approach learning give strong support to the hypothesis suggested by prior research that students with positive attitudes towards learning are much more likely to invest in effective learning strategies. A particularly strong feature of this relationship is the association between believing in one's own efficacy as a learner and controlling one's own learning. The PISA results show striking similarities across countries in the pattern of relationships between different characteristics of students as learners.

- Strong student attitudes towards learning are associated with strong performance partly through their link with use of learning strategies, but also after controlling for this factor. For example, students interested in reading show higher reading literacy levels regardless of how much they think about and control what they are learning. On the other hand, students motivated by external factors like getting a good job perform better only where they have other strengths, such as controlling their learning.

- On average, about one-fifth of the variation in student reading literacy performance in each country can be explained by differences in approaches to learning. About two-thirds of variation in students' tendency to control their learning can be explained by differences in their levels of motivation and self-related beliefs. Thus while students' learning approaches are just some among many factors that can influence cognitive outcomes, positive student attitudes are central to developing strong, self-managed learning techniques. The latter is desirable as an outcome in itself — as a precondition to lifelong learning.

Introduction

Careful analysis of the results of PISA 2000 shows that when students in different countries answered questions about their motivation, their self-related beliefs and their learning strategies, they were describing comparable concepts irrespective of their cultural background[1]. This important finding confirms that PISA results can be used to explore how various aspects of student approaches to learning are related to each other and to student performance in different countries. This chapter explores such relationships. Note that the ability to compare how different student characteristics interact *within* various countries is not the same as being able to compare the strength of an individual characteristic such as student motivation *across* countries. The latter kind of comparison, possible to a more limited extent, is explored in Chapter 3.

This chapter considers, in turn, four types of relationship. First, it looks at how particular aspects of student approaches to learning are associated with student performance in the PISA reading literacy assessment. Second, it looks at how these different aspects relate to each other. Third, it considers the relative importance of different aspects in relation to performance, when taking into account the interaction between them. Finally, it asks how much of the variation in students' reading literacy performance and in their tendency to control their learning can be explained by the combination of a selection of the characteristics of students as learners that are measured by PISA.

Student approaches to learning and student performance

As outlined in Chapter 1, students who approach learning with strong motivation, with a belief in themselves and with a range of learning strategies are more likely than other students to perform well at school. PISA looked at several characteristics within each of these categories of student approaches and confirmed that these factors are associated with measured performance. To illustrate such relationships, the following analysis looks at one indicative characteristic within each category:

- The use of *control strategies* is used to illustrate how learning strategies are associated with performance. Thinking about what one needs to learn and relating this to learning goals is a particularly important aspect of regulating one's own learning, which prior research has shown to have a particularly close association with performance.

- The link between motivation and performance is illustrated by *interest in reading*, one of the motivational characteristics measured, which is another good predictor of how well students read.

- *Self-efficacy* or the belief by students in their ability to handle learning tasks even if they find them difficult, is used to illustrate how students' self-related beliefs and their performance are related. Self-efficacy goes beyond how good students think they are in subjects such as reading and is more concerned with the kind of confidence that is needed for them to take on learning tasks that they find challenging. It is therefore not simply a reflection of a student's abilities and performance and is particularly likely to enhance learning activity, which in turn improves reading literacy.

Figures 2.1 to 2.3 show the relationship of each of these three characteristics with performance in reading. They do so in each case by dividing students into four groups according to their performance on the relevant scale. The average reading literacy score of students in each of the four groups is shown for each country. Countries are ranked by the length of the line connecting these scores – that is, the performance gap between the bottom and top quarter of students on each scale. Thus in countries to the left of each graph, the relationship between the relevant characteristic and student reading literacy is the strongest.

An overall finding is that in all countries in all three categories the students with the most "positive" characteristics perform significantly better than those with the least positive. In all but a few cases, the gap between the quarters of the population with the highest- and lowest-rated learner characteristics is between 30 and 100 points on the reading literacy scale. The magnitude of these differences can be understood in several ways:

• In terms of the difficulty of tasks that students can do. PISA reading tasks of ascending difficulty, from the most basic to very complex, were associated with five levels of proficiency in PISA. Thirty points on the scale represents just under half a proficiency level; 100 points is nearly one and a half levels. Thus for example, in Portugal, the quarter of students who control their learning the most (Figure 2.1) are able on average to perform reading literacy tasks near the middle of Level 3 (medium difficulty), whereas the quarter who do so least can only cope with much more basic tasks near the bottom of Level 2.

• In relation to the overall distribution of student reading literacy scores. One hundred points represents one standard deviation, which means that two-thirds of the OECD student population have scores within 100 points of the OECD mean.

Figure 2.1

Performance on the combined reading literacy scale, by national quarters of the student population according to how much they use CONTROL STRATEGIES

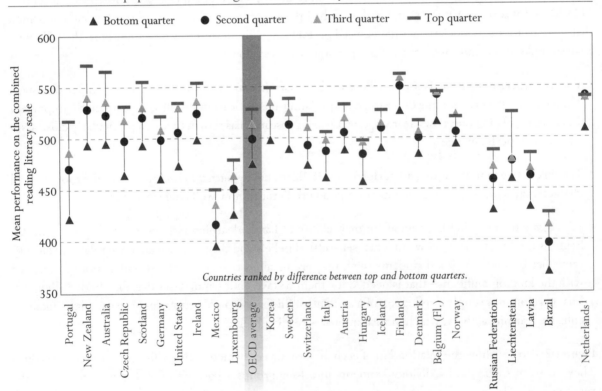

1. Response rate is too low to ensure comparability.
Source: OECD PISA Database, 2001. Table C2.2.

• In relation to average student performance in different countries. All but two OECD countries have mean reading literacy scores within a range of 76 points. Differences associated with student approaches to learning can be large by comparison. For example, the students in the bottom quarter on interest in reading in Germany have a mean score that is lower than the mean score of students in all OECD countries except Luxembourg and Mexico, whereas the quarter of Germans with greatest reading interest have a mean score higher than the whole student population in even the best-performing country.

Thus there are important differences between the performance of students with more and less favourable characteristics in terms of strategies, motivation and self-related beliefs. However, to put this in perspective, one must bear in mind that these are only some among many factors associated with variations in performance and a particular strength on one of these characteristics alone might therefore be a relatively weak predictor of how well a student will perform. This is especially so across countries, where not only does the relative advantage associated with a characteristic vary, but this advantage is also related to different mean performance overall. Thus, for example, as shown in Figure 2.1, the quarter of students who control their learning the most in Luxembourg and Mexico have lower average reading literacy performance than those who control it the least in 12 other OECD countries.

Figure 2.2

Performance on the combined reading literacy scale, by national quarters of the student population according to how much they are INTERESTED IN READING

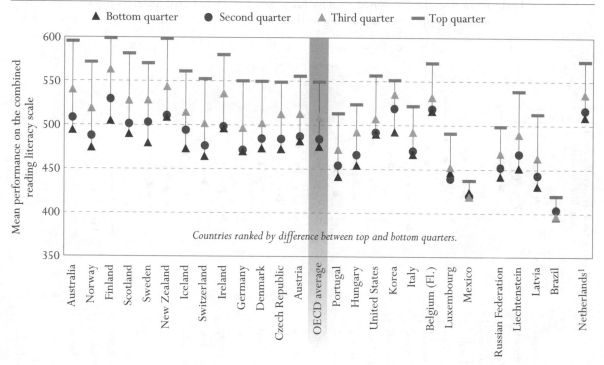

1. Response rate is too low to ensure comparability.
Source: OECD PISA Database, 2001. Table C2.3.

Looking specifically at each of these effects:

• The use of control strategies (Figure 2.1) is most closely associated with reading literacy in Portugal, with a gap of 96 points between more and less frequent users of these strategies. The difference exceeds 60 points, almost one proficiency level, in Australia, Germany, New Zealand, the Czech Republic, Liechtenstein, Scotland and the United States. The lowest gap, in Norway and Belgium (Fl.) is under 30 points, but still substantial.

• The difference in reading literacy performance between students with the greatest *interest in reading* and those with the least interest is, on average in OECD countries, one full proficiency level or 74 points (Figure 2.2). This makes it the strongest predictor overall of performance among the factors looked at here. It is highest in Australia and Norway, with a gap of around 100 points and 45 points or more in all OECD countries except Mexico.

Students who believe in their own *efficacy* are also more likely on average to perform well in reading literacy (Figure 2.3). This advantage is greatest in Denmark, Iceland and Sweden, with a gap of 80 and more points. It is smallest in Belgium (Fl.), Hungary, Italy and the Netherlands, at below 40 points.

Figure 2.3

Performance on the combined reading literacy scale, by national quarters of the student population according to their SELF-EFFICACY BELIEFS

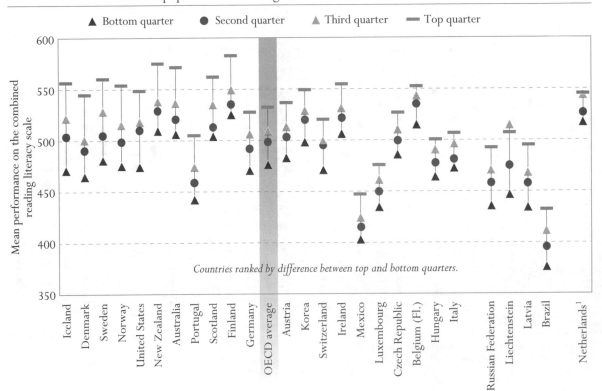

1. Response rate is too low to ensure comparability.
Source: OECD PISA Database, 2001. Table C2.4.

In addition to these performance differences between the quarter of students with the most and the quarter with the least favourable characteristics, Figures 2.1 to 2.3 produce some interesting findings when looking also at the gaps between scores in all four quarters. For example, there are cases where there is little difference between the bottom two or three quarters and others where there is a cluster at the top. These patterns are significant because they indicate whether each factor is important for a relatively small minority of underachieving students; or conversely whether only a minority of students with particularly strong approaches to learning excel in this respect. This can help policy makers to decide whether remedial measures should focus on a narrower or wider section of the student population.

In the case of control strategies, students in the two medium categories have similar performance in most countries, with an average gap of only 14 points in OECD countries. The main distinctions are thus between those reporting high, medium (middle half of the student population) and low use of such strategies. In some countries, most notably Belgium (Fl.), Finland and the Netherlands, there is little distinction among high and medium users of control strategies: it is only those using them the least who have lower performance. This suggests that students in these countries who think about what they need to learn and check their own progress at least a minimum amount perform better than those who do these things rarely or not at all, but that beyond this minimum more frequent use of control does not make a difference.

In the case of reading interest, in contrast, the greatest distinction in performance is between the quarter of students with the highest interest and the rest. In almost all countries, the differences between students in the bottom two categories are small. In some, notably Belgium (Fl.), Luxembourg, Mexico and the United States, the performance means of students in each of the lowest three quarters by reading interest almost coincide. In most other countries, the gap between the top two quarters is larger than between the bottom two: the only exceptions are the Czech Republic, Finland, Hungary, Korea and Sweden. Thus it is a keen interest in reading that most distinguishes students with good reading performance and policy interventions that only raised reading interest from low to moderate might have limited effect.

In the case of students ranked by their beliefs in their efficacy, differences in performance between the middle categories are again small. In most countries, both very low belief and very high beliefs in one's efficacy are associated with differences in performance from the norm.

How do student approaches to learning relate to each other?

Even though motivation, self beliefs and learning strategies describe different aspects of learner behaviour and attitudes, they are often mutually dependent. However, previous research on these relationships has not made it clear to what extent they are similar or different across countries. An analysis of such similarities and differences is of particular interest because patterns of learning approaches can suggest potential ways of helping and encouraging students to regulate their own learning and illustrate students' perceptions of their learning environment.

A central hypothesis in the study of learning strategies, backed by considerable research evidence, is that students are most likely to initiate high quality learning, using various strategies, if they are well motivated and believe in their own capacities. In particular, research has identified close relationships between interest in learning and the use of deep processing strategies – the elaboration strategies measured in PISA, involving the student in relating new information to prior knowledge (Baumert and Köller, 1998). There are good grounds for this. The use of comprehension-oriented forms of learning is time- and effort-intensive. It involves the explicit checking of relations between previously acquired knowledge and new information, the formulation of hypotheses about possible connections and the testing of these hypotheses against the background of the new material. For this reason, learners are only willing to invest such effort if they have a strong interest in a subject or if there is a considerable benefit, in terms of high performance, with learners motivated by the external reward of performing well (Hatano, 1998). This applies both to the use of deeper processes of comprehension (elaboration) and to the identification of gaps in one's own comprehension (control). This helps explain the close observed connection between interest/motivation and strategy use.

Figure 2.4 illustrates the connection by considering two aspects of motivation and one of self-related beliefs, in terms of their association with the use of two of the strategies that students were asked about in PISA. Although the direction of the arrows reflects prior evidence that such associations are linked to the importance of motivation and self-confidence as preconditions to investment in learning strategies, PISA does not provide direct evidence that they *cause* such investment.

Figure 2.4

How student motivation and self-related beliefs are associated with the learning strategies that they adopt

The **width of each arrow is proportional to the** *correlation coefficient* shown in each box, which indicates the strength of association on a scale ranging from zero for no simple association to 1 for perfect correlation (or -1 if the relationship is negative). The proportion of variation in student use of learning strategies associated with each factor shown is equal to the square of the correlation coefficient. Thus for example around a quarter of the differences in the extent to which students use control strategies is associated with differences in how much they believe in their own efficacy. **The direction of the arrows in this diagram indicate a suggested effect rather than a demonstrated causal link.** The correlations coefficients shown are the means of the coefficients for each country.

Source: OECD PISA Database, 2001. Tables C2.5a and C2.5c.

The use of control strategies tends to be more time-consuming than memorisation and thus can be expected to depend more on strong motivation and self-confidence. This is indeed shown in the PISA findings, particularly for interest in reading, which has little association with the adoption of memorisation strategies. However, repetition-based memorisation is also dependent on learner motivation. Students who aspire to a particular occupation and orient their learning activities around this goal – who are instrumentally motivated – are more likely than other students to use different learning strategies, to about an equal extent in the case of control and memorisation. Students benefit strongly if they believe in their own efficacy as learners and the results in Figure 2.4 show that those who have such belief are particularly likely to adopt strategies to control their learning. This association is stronger than the ones between learning strategies and reading interest or instrumental motivation.

Figure 2.5

Correlation[1] between aspects of motivation, self-related beliefs
and student use of CONTROL STRATEGIES

■   Self-efficacy
▲   Instrumental motivation
◆   Interest in reading

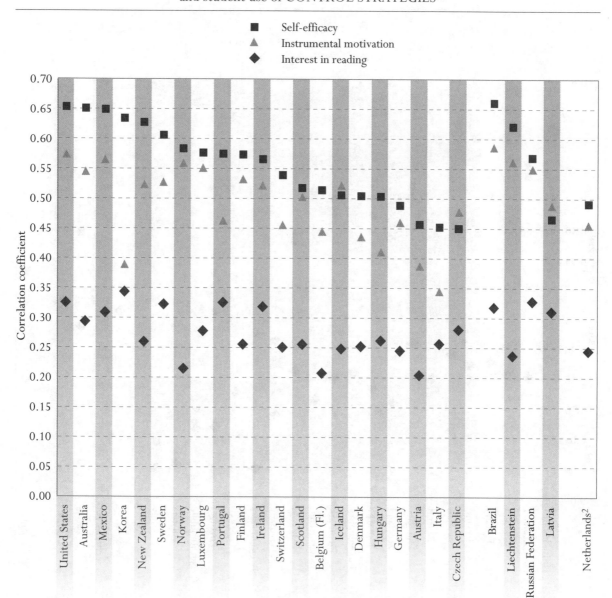

1. Based on simple associations between pairs of variables (bivariate correlations).
2. Response rate is too low to ensure comparability.
Source: OECD PISA Database, 2001. Table C2.5c.

To what extent are these observations true in individual countries? Figures 2.5 and 2.6 show the strength of the six correlations in Figure 2.4 in each country (and Tables C2.5a-j show more comprehensively the strength of correlation between pairs of the learner attributes measured in PISA). Patterns are relatively consistent across countries and in particular the more high cost strategies are everywhere associated with motivation and self-related beliefs.

Figure 2.6

Correlation[1] between aspects of motivation, self-related beliefs and
student use of MEMORISATION STRATEGIES

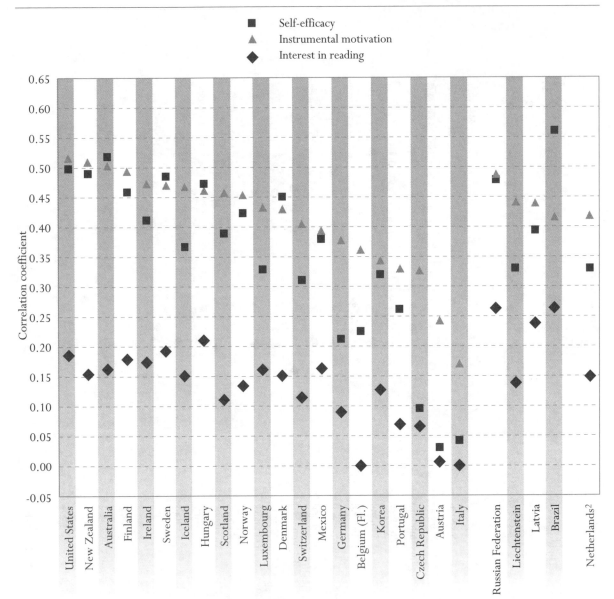

1. Based on simple associations between pairs of variables (bivariate correlations).
2. Response rate is too low to ensure comparability.
Source: OECD PISA Database, 2001. Table C2.5a.

For example, the correlation between self-efficacy and control strategies is in every country at least 0.45. In
Australia, Brazil, Korea, Liechtenstein, Mexico, New Zealand, Sweden and the United States it is above 0.6.
Instrumental motivation is somewhat less closely associated with control strategies in all countries except
the Czech Republic, Iceland and Latvia, but the correlation exceeds 0.4 in all countries except Austria,
Italy and Korea. Correlations between interest in reading and use of control strategies range from 0.2
(Austria) to 0.34 (Korea), indicating a lower, moderate level of association.

The use of memorisation strategies is most strongly associated with instrumental motivation, with a correlation coefficient above 0.3 everywhere except Austria and Italy. The association with self-efficacy is slightly lower in most countries and only greater in Australia, Brazil, Denmark, Hungary and Sweden. In general, students with a more pronounced interest in reading do not report much greater use of memorisation strategies, with correlations below 0.1 in several countries.

Figures 2.4 to 2.6 cover only four of the 11 characteristics of motivation, self-related beliefs and learning strategies measured in PISA. Data on mutual relationships between all these characteristics, shown in Annex C (Tables C2.5a-j), shows that the strongest relationships are:

* between students' views of their own efficacy and the effort and persistence that they are willing to exert; and

* between each of these two characteristics and students' use of control strategies.

The above findings suggest two overall conclusions:

* Any attempts to foster self-regulated learning need to address both the strategies students adopt to process information and the way in which students appraise themselves and are motivated to learn. In particular, students need to have confidence in themselves and to believe it is worth putting in effort to achieve particular goals if they are to take control of their own learning.

* These relationships apply across countries and thus raise similar issues across education systems. The correlations shown in Figures 2.5 and 2.6 are strikingly similar across countries and even where there are differences, the general pattern of these relationships is homogeneous. Certainly no country can afford to ignore the associations between students' attitudes to learning and their behaviour in adopting effective learning strategies.

Separating out the effect of each factor

The analysis up to here has looked at whether students who have certain characteristics are more likely to perform well in reading literacy and whether those with stronger motivation or self-related beliefs are more likely to adopt particular learning strategies. However, the interactions between all these factors make it difficult to separate out the effect of any one of them. For example, students who say that they are interested in reading are also more likely to perform well. But they are also more likely to believe in their own efficacy and to exert effort and persistence, factors also associated with strong performance. To what extent is being keen on reading a predictor, in itself, of good performance and to what extent can the high performance of keen readers be explained by the fact that they also tend to have these other positive attributes?

By building a model of the multiple interaction among these variables, it is possible to separate out the impact of each – effectively looking at the association between, say, reading interest and performance while controlling for other measured characteristics. This makes it possible to distinguish a separate effect for each variable.

The model used here to analyse these effects considers the three characteristics used in the previous section to measure motivation and self-related beliefs, alongside students' use of control strategies and their reading literacy performance. It assumes that (*i*) belief in one's own efficacy, (*ii*) extrinsic or instrumental motivation and (*iii*) intrinsic motivation as represented by interest in reading, are drivers which initiate investment in learning activity, with the adoption of particular strategies represented in the model by students' tendency to control their own learning. Further, it assumes that students' performance in reading literacy can be predicted by the direct effect of attributes (*i*) to (*iii*), as well as by the frequency with which students use control strategies. The latter serves as a mediating variable, to the extent that the effects of motivation and self-confidence on performance operate via the tendency of well-motivated students to use control strategies and hence perform better in the assessment.

Figure 2.7

Individual factors associated with control strategies and performance, when controlling for other factors

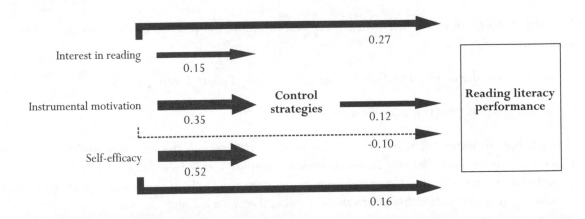

The width of each arrow is proportional to the *regression coefficient,* shown in each box, a measure of the association between the factors comparable in meaning to that shown in Figure 2.4 above (however, the proportion of explained variance cannot in this case be calculated from the coefficient for a single variable, since several variables are looked at simultaneously). *The direction of the arrows in this diagram indicate a suggested effect rather than a demonstrated causal link.*

Source: OECD PISA Database, 2001. Table C2.7a.

The methodology[2] used here involves testing the extent to which the assumed relationships in this model are confirmed by the observed relationships. Figure 2.7 shows the measured degree of association for each of the relationships in the model. These are different from the measures used earlier in this chapter in that in each case they separate out the specific effect by controlling for relationships with other variables. In the case of the strongest association, between self-efficacy and control strategies, this does not make much difference: students who believe in their own efficacy are much more likely to take control of their own learning regardless of their other characteristics. However, the separate associations between the two motivational factors and control strategies are more modest and somewhat weaker than the simple (bivariate) relationships shown in Figure 2.4.

Again, these results are fairly consistent across countries (see Tables C2.6 and C2.7a,b). In all OECD countries the association between self-efficacy and control strategies is relatively high, with regression coefficients between 0.41 and 0.61 except in Korea, where it is 0.74. Only in Iceland and Latvia is students' instrumental motivation a stronger predictor than their beliefs in their own efficacy or whether they use control strategies. In these countries, students who aspire to concrete occupational goals and who gear their learning to achieving them are particularly likely to control their own learning activity. In all countries other than Italy, Korea and Mexico this latter effect is relatively high, with a regression coefficient above 0.3. On the other hand, having an interest in reading is not a strong separate predictor of whether students control their learning, once other characteristics of keen readers are taken into account. In this case the coefficient is above 0.2 only in the Czech Republic, Germany, Italy and the Netherlands. Thus, being intrinsically motivated through subject interest does not appear to be a very important influence on whether students invest in powerful learning strategies in the absence of other influences, such as confidence by the student that the strategy will pay off because they are good at learning.

Figure 2.7 also looks at the separate association of various student characteristics with performance in the PISA assessment. At the beginning of this chapter, it was shown that the quarter of students with stronger characteristics as learners perform better than the quarter with weaker ones. Figure 2.7 shows the degree to which students with each characteristic perform better, controlling for the fact that they are also likely to have positive scores on other characteristics. The model assumes that:

(*i*) Individual aspects of student motivation and self-related beliefs have direct effects on performance, beyond any association with other such aspects or with student learning strategies. The strength of such associations is shown by the arrows crossing Figure 2.7. They show that students who are interested in reading tend to be good readers regardless of other aspects of their attitudes or behaviour: this factor is the strongest single predictor of performance in 15 countries. Overall the predictive power of self-efficacy for students' reading performance is the strongest in Denmark, Iceland and Norway. And in the Czech Republic, Italy, Luxembourg, Mexico and New Zealand control strategies have the highest direct effect (see Table C2.7a). However, when other factors are taken into account, instrumental motivation has on average no clear association with performance: in some countries there is a negative relationship. This finding should be interpreted with caution. It does not mean that being motivated by external factors such as a desire to get a good job may cause worse performance at school: the fact that students with these characteristics are more likely to use effective learning strategies clearly contradicts such an interpretation. Rather, it may arise because of the composition of the group of students most likely to be thinking about the labour market at age 15. These tend to be students considering leaving education soon rather than progressing to academic tracks, whose academic performance is on average lower.

(*ii*) Adopting a particular learning strategy affects performance, independently of the fact that students with strong learning strategies also tend to be well motivated and confident of their own abilities. In fact, this association in the case of control strategies is on average very modest and in some countries cannot be discerned at all. This is not because controlling one's learning does not help performance, but rather because such a large amount of the variation in the degree to which students control their learning is associated with variation in their motivation and self-related beliefs (see Figure 2.7 and Table C2.7b).

(*iii*) Some of the effect of self-confidence and strong motivation is in fact mediated by the use of effective learning strategies. For example, a student who is strongly motivated by external success is also more likely to put effort into controlling learning by checking that goals have been met and this in turn improves the chance of good performance. The overall strength of association between each factor and performance, a total effect combining direct and mediated effects, is shown in Table C2.7b. The degree to which learning strategies mediate the effect on performance of student attitudes appears to be greatest in the case of self-efficacy, for which the total effect is 0.23 compared to a direct effect of 0.16. This is particularly so for Mexico, New Zealand and Portugal where, other things equal, students who believe in their own efficacy are no more likely to perform well, but are markedly more likely to do so once one takes account of their greater investment in control strategies. The total contribution of the individual factors shown in Figure 2.7 is further analysed in the following section.

The factors in combination: How much do these characteristics together explain differences in student performance and the use of control strategies?

It is clear from the above that while the separate effects of individual student characteristics on student performance and on the use of control strategies are not always great, measurement of the overall effect is different from the sum of these individual associations, since several factors may combine to have an influence. The modelling process allows the combined effect of several characteristics to be measured by considering the percentage of variation in, for example, student performance that could be explained by the combined association with related factors. These results are shown in Figure 2.8.

Figure 2.8

The combined explanatory power of student characteristics on
(A) performance outcomes and (B) control of learning

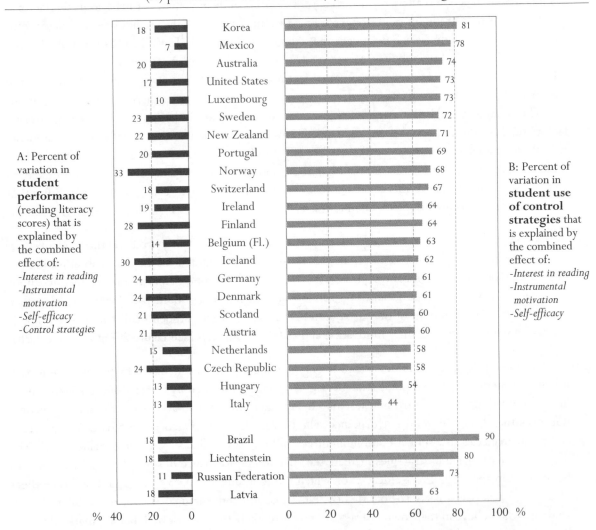

A: Percent of variation in **student performance** (reading literacy scores) that is explained by the combined effect of:
-*Interest in reading*
-*Instrumental motivation*
-*Self-efficacy*
-*Control strategies*

B: Percent of variation in **student use of control strategies** that is explained by the combined effect of:
-*Interest in reading*
-*Instrumental motivation*
-*Self-efficacy*

Note: The numbers indicate r² (the proportion of variance in student performance or student use of control strategies explained by student characteristics) for each part of the model.
Source: OECD PISA Database, 2001. Tables C2.6 and C2.8.

The striking finding here is the very high degree to which the amount that students control their learning is associated with a combination of their interest in reading, their instrumental motivation and their beliefs in their own efficacy. In all countries other than Italy these factors explain most of the difference and in Brazil, Korea, Liechtenstein and Mexico it is over three quarters. This lends strong support for the hypothesis that students will only control their learning if they are well motivated and or have strong beliefs in their abilities. Since control of the learning process is to some extent an outcome in its own right, helping students to become autonomous lifelong learners, this finding is important. It suggests that in all countries, adopting an effective learning strategy depends not just on having cognitive tools (knowing how to learn) but also on having certain attitudes and dispositions (wanting to learn).

While students' attitudes can thus explain most differences in one outcome, controlling the learning process, the learner characteristics explain only part of the variation in student performance. The proportion of variance in reading literacy explained by these factors exceeds 25 per cent only in Finland, Iceland and Norway and is on average about one-fifth. However, given the many known and unknown influences on student performance, this degree of association still indicates that large and valuable gains could be made in the performance of weaker students if stronger approaches to learning could be fostered.

In considering how these factors relate to other influences on student performance, it is worth noting that if family background factors are added to the model, the total amount of explained variance rises only slightly (see Table C2.8). This is because, even though family background has been found to be strongly associated with performance, it is also associated with strong student approaches to learning (see Chapter 4). Thus knowing the background of a student does not add much to one's power to predict their performance if one already knows about their motivation, self-related beliefs and use of learning strategies.

But this also raises the question of whether characteristics such as strong motivation are indeed exerting an influence on performance, or whether it is just that strongly motivated students happen to have advantaged backgrounds which help them to perform well regardless of how they approach learning. This question can be answered by controlling for family background and looking at the unique[3] effects of particular characteristics (see Table C2.8). In fact, the effects of approaches to learning do not disappear and remain particularly strong for interest in reading. Indeed, in Denmark, Finland, Iceland, Ireland, Korea, Latvia, New Zealand, Norway, Scotland and Sweden, the unique effect of student interest in reading is even greater than that of family background.

Summary of key findings and their implications

The implications of the main findings in this chapter, which will be revisited in the policy discussion in Chapter 5, can be summarised as follows:

• While students with stronger approaches to learning are generally shown by PISA to perform better, the distribution of performance is not even. In particular, it appears that the greatest benefit from increased use of control strategies could be gained from those students who use them least rather than moving from moderate to much higher use. On the other hand moving from minimal to moderate interest in reading may have limited effect, since only the keenest readers tend to perform much better. This has implications for the targeting of interventions.

• Student learning strategies are closely associated with their attitudes to learning and to their own abilities. This applies both to students' investment in sophisticated strategies such as controlling the learning process and to more basic functions like remembering what one learns. In the case of the former, belief in one's own efficacy is particularly important, for the latter, students who are motivated by instrumental goals such as job success are most likely to be strong. Thus the nurturing of a range of positive attitudes can help develop rounded learners and this has implications for policy across OECD countries, since the effects described are remarkably similar across a range of cultural settings.

- While being keen on learning for its own sake – for example being interested in reading – does not on its own have a strong link with particular learning strategies, its link with performance independent of strategy use is stronger than any other variables measured. Thus while self-confidence and motivation for instrumental ends may be important to develop so that students will find it worth investing in effective learning strategies, encouraging a love of learning is a separate way of helping students towards better performance.

- Overall, very strong links between student attitudes and learning behaviours suggest that motivation and self-confidence are indispensable to outcomes that will foster lifelong learning. The combined effect on control strategies suggest that teaching a student how to learn autonomously is unlikely to work without strong motivation and self-confidence.

- Different student approaches to learning are closely associated with the disparities in learning outcomes of students from different family backgrounds. The high amount of shared variance between students' family background and their approaches to learning indicates that the effect of having an advantaged family background can, to a large extent, be more precisely specified as being more likely to use control strategies, believe in one's efficacy and be well motivated. And even after controlling for family background, students with effective approaches to learning outperform their peers with less effective approaches in terms of performance. Thus fostering more positive approaches to learning can be an important part of schools' efforts to reduce the impact.

Notes

1. This conclusion is based on analysis of patterns of interaction between various characteristics observed, to ensure "structural equivalence" of the reported scales. Annex B explains this technical analysis and its findings.

2. Structural equation modelling – explained in Annex D. For the sake of simplicity, Figure 2.7 only displays the structural part of the model. The calculation was performed with a complete measurement model.

3. In this case an even more "conservative" test of the separate effects of each variable is used than in the earlier "structural equation" model. This controls also for "confounded" effects.

COMPARING COUNTRIES: PROFILES OF STUDENT APPROACHES TO LEARNING

KEY POINTS

- Direct comparisons of the average strength in different countries of student approaches to learning are possible for only five of the 13 characteristics measured in PISA. For the rest, the absence across countries of positive relationships between learner characteristics and performance, which exist within countries, suggests that students from different cultures are not describing the strength of their approaches in directly comparable terms.

- For the five characteristics that can be compared (use of memorisation, verbal and mathematical self-concept, self-efficacy and preference for co-operative learning), important differences are observed among students from various countries. For example, in every country students are more confident in their verbal than their mathematical abilities, but to a greatly varying extent from one country to another.

- When the student population is divided into four roughly equal groups with similar sets of characteristics, one cluster with generally strong approaches to learning performs considerably better than another cluster with generally weak approaches. The difference between these groups is on average about one proficiency level in reading literacy. Two middle groups, one with stronger than average characteristics overall but below-average in attitudes to mathematics and the other the converse, tend to be fairly close together in their reading literacy performance. These patterns are broadly similar across countries.

- Differences between the characteristics of students as learners in different countries and between students in different schools within countries, account for only a small part of the variation in approaches to learning. The most important source of this variation lies within schools, each of which contains stronger and weaker learners.

Introduction

This chapter provides participating countries with feedback on their students' approaches to learning. It considers the extent to which students at the end of compulsory schooling have characteristics that help them to learn successfully and in particular to regulate their own learning effectively. As noted in Chapter 1, these characteristics are important as outcomes of schooling in their own right, as preconditions to lifelong learning, as well as contributing to students' acquisition of knowledge and skills while at school.

The analysis considers the incidence of all 13 characteristics described in Figure 1.1. These include the 11 characteristics used to measure attributes associated with students' capacity to regulate their own learning (motivation, self-related beliefs and use of learning strategies), as well as the two others that consider students' learning preferences – for co-operative and for competitive learning situations.

While Chapter 2 was able to observe differences between students with more or less positive approaches to learning within each country, student characteristics across countries need to be compared with caution. Analysis of the results shows that the average strengths of student learning approaches in different countries cannot always be legitimately compared on the basis of how students describe their attitudes and behaviours when answering the PISA questionnaire. This chapter discusses in turn:

• Which aspects of student approaches to learning allow comparison of average scores across cultural contexts and which do not.

• How student approaches compare across countries in those respects for which comparisons are valid.

• The distribution among students of the various learner characteristics measured by PISA. This analysis looks at the extent to which stronger or weaker characteristics are concentrated among certain students, to create clusters of students with similar sets of attributes. The extent of this clustering effect can be compared across countries.

• Overall, the degree to which variations in student learning approaches occur across countries, across schools or across individuals.

In what respects can the average strength of student learning approaches be compared across countries?

Can asking students in different countries about their learning attitudes and behaviours produce comparable information on how students actually approach learning from one education system to another? This depends on how students in different cultures answer questions about themselves. For example, do Korean students mean the same as Brazilian students when they say that they put great effort and persistence into learning? There are good reasons to assume that this will not always be the case, due to different cultural norms with respect to things such as modesty and self-assertion. Research evidence confirms that self-reported characteristics are vulnerable to such problems of comparability across cultures (*e.g.,* Heine *et al*, 1999; van de Vijver and Leung, 1997; Bempechat, Jimenez and Boulay, 2002). A particular difficulty has been encountered when comparing collectively and individualistically oriented societies, such as Japan and the United States.

Close analysis of the answers given by students in the PISA survey, combined with the results of the assessment of their performance, shows:

• That when students in different countries reported on their motivation, self-related beliefs, learning strategies and learning preferences in the PISA 2000 survey, they were at least reporting on comparable concepts. This finding, based on analysis of the patterns of results in various countries[1], makes it possible to compare certain relationships within one country with the same relationships in another. Thus, for example, Chapter 2 was legitimately able to compare the strength of association between student motivation and student performance in the different countries taking part in PISA.

• That there are positive relationships within every country between most of the student characteristics assumed to help learning (measuring motivation, self-related beliefs and use of learning strategies) and student performance (reading literacy). This establishes a firm relationship, valid throughout the PISA countries, between approaches to learning and performance. Within-country comparisons are the most reliable test of this relationship since they compare answers given by students from within a broadly similar cultural setting.

• That such a relationship is not always produced by comparing average student scores for countries. For example, Korean students have a tendency to say that they do not have a strong interest in reading, whereas Brazilian students are inclined to say that they do. Yet the average Korean student can tackle a medium to difficult reading task near the top of Proficiency Level 3, whereas the average Brazilian student can only tackle very basic tasks near the top of Level 1. Figure 3.1 shows that in countries where students say they have higher reading interest, they do not necessarily perform better overall. Indeed, despite the fact that

| Figure 3.1 |

Interest in reading and performance on the combined reading literacy scale

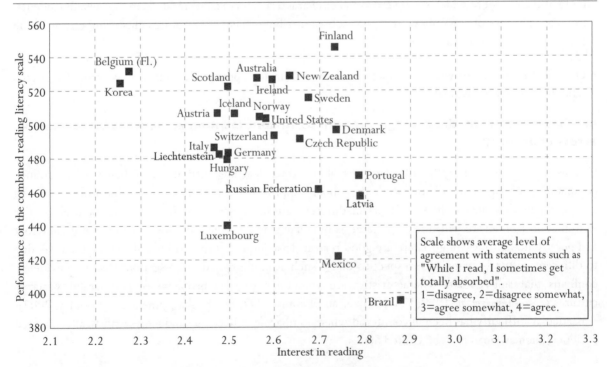

Note: This graph illustrates the difficulty of comparing self-reported learning approaches across countries. Within-country comparisons show that students who are more interested in reading have HIGHER average reading literacy.

Source: OECD PISA Database, 2001. Tables C3.1a and C3.1b.

in a country such as Finland, where there is no consistent cross-country relationship, reading interest and performance are both high, overall.

Given that within-country comparisons show a clear association between student interest and performance, this cross-country result can be taken to demonstrate that students' expressions of the strength of their interest in reading in different countries is anchored around different norms. It is possible, for example, that a level of interest in reading described by a Korean student as moderate is described by a Brazilian student as a keen interest. Even though the meaning of interest in reading is interpreted by Korean and Brazilian students in similar ways, the anchoring of the scale thus differs. So it is not valid to compare the average reading interest of Brazilian students and Korean students. But one can still compare within-country differences in reading interest: for example, how much more interested female students are than male students in Korea, as compared with the equivalent gender difference in Brazil (see Chapter 4).

• For eight of the 13 PISA scales measuring learner characteristics, careful analysis shows that as with interest in reading, it is not appropriate to compare average student scores across countries (see Annex B). In all of these cases, characteristics that are positively associated with performance within countries show negative associations in comparison across countries. A notable feature of these results is that Brazilian students, who were assessed as having the lowest mean literacy performance of the 32 countries in PISA 2000, report the strongest learner characteristics on four of the eight scales: they say that they are more interested in reading, are more interested in mathematics, put in more effort and use comprehension-oriented learning strategies (elaboration) more than is claimed in any other country. Conversely, Korean students, whose mean reading literacy performance can be said with confidence to be above that of students in at least 23 of the other 31 countries in the assessment, report lower mean scores than any other country on each of the four PISA measures of motivation: interest in reading, interest in mathematics, instrumental motivation and effort and persistence.

The strength of the following eight student attributes **cannot** be directly compared across cultures:

• Use of elaboration strategies
• Use of control strategies
• Instrumental motivation
• Interest in reading
• Interest in mathematics
• Effort and persistence
• Academic self-concept
• Preference for competitive learning

• For the other five learning-related characteristics measured in PISA, these difficulties in comparability across countries do not arise. In these cases, the relationship between learner characteristics and performance follows similar patterns within and across countries (see Table B2.5) and therefore it can be considered valid to compare the mean strength of these characteristics cross-nationally. One must nevertheless interpret these comparisons, presented in the following section, with some caution. For example, overall there is a slight negative correlation at the country level between beliefs in one's own efficacy and performance; however, this result can primarily be attributed to the results in just three countries. In Brazil and Mexico, students believe strongly in their efficacy but perform badly; Korean students believe weakly in their efficacy but perform well.

The strength of the following five student attributes **can** be directly compared across cultures:

• Use of memorisation strategies
• Self-concept in reading
• Mathematical self-concept
• Self-efficacy
• Preference for co-operative learning

International comparison of the student learning characteristics

Of the five student characteristics of learning that can be compared across countries, one relates to learning strategies, three to students' self-related beliefs and the fifth to their approaches to learning. Due to the problems with comparability of the strength of student attributes explored in the previous section, there are no straightforward ways of comparing the strength of student motivation from one country to another.

Learning strategy

Differences across countries in the degree to which students say that they use particular learning strategies are more pronounced in the case of ***memorisation*** than the other strategies looked at in PISA (Tables C3.1 and C3.2) and this is also the only strategy where country comparisons are not problematic. Figure 3.2 summarises the degree to which students report that they frequently draw on memorisation, try to memorise everything covered in school, memorise new material and practice by saying the material to themselves over and over. Students in Hungary in particular use memorisation most frequently, along with those in Scotland and the Russian Federation; students in Italy and Norway do so least frequently. In interpreting these differences, one should note that memorisation shows a less consistent association with performance than the other two strategies (control and elaboration) examined in PISA. Although in some countries, including Hungary and the Russian Federation where memorisation is strong overall, students using these strategies perform significantly better, in about half there was no discernible effect. In four countries, including Italy where use of memorisation is weak, students using it more tend to have weaker performance. This does not however show that memorisation strategies never contribute to effective learning: rather, where weaker readers memorise more, they may do so to make up for other learning limitations.

Figure 3.2

Student use of memorisation strategies

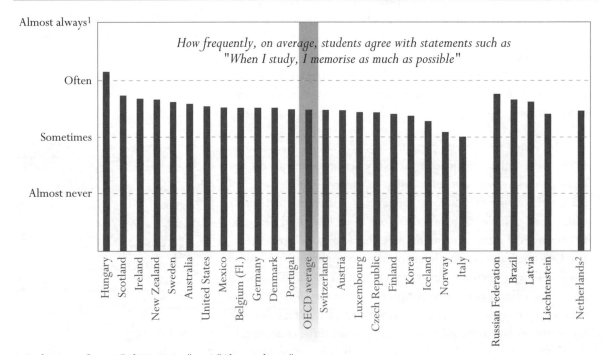

1. Scale ranges from 1 "Almost never" to 4 "Almost always".
2. Response rate is too low to ensure comparability.
Source: OECD PISA Database, 2001. Table C3.2.

Self-related beliefs

Three of the five comparisons that can be made across countries relate to the strength of students' beliefs in themselves. At one level, it is not surprising that students who perform well in PISA also tend to have high opinions of themselves, yet as explained in Box C, self-regard must be seen as much more than simply a mirror of student performance: rather, it can have a decisive influence on the learning process. Whether students choose to pursue a particular learning goal is dependent on their appraisal of their abilities and potential in a subject domain and on their confidence on being able to achieve this goal even in the face of difficulties. These two features of self-related beliefs are considered in turn below.

Box C. Do students' beliefs about their abilities simply mirror their performance?

One issue that arises when asking students what they think of their own abilities, especially in terms of whether they can perform verbal and mathematical tasks which are also assessed directly in PISA, is whether this adds anything important to what we know about their abilities from the assessment. In fact, both prior research and the PISA results give strong reasons for assuming that confidence helps *drive* learning success, rather than simply *reflecting* it. In particular:

- Research about the learning process has shown that students need to believe in their own capacities before making necessary investments in learning strategies that will help them to higher performance (see Zimmerman, 1999). This finding is also supported by PISA: Figure 2.7 shows that the beliefs in one's efficacy are a particularly strong predictor of whether a student will control his or her learning.

- Much more of the observed variation in student levels of self-related beliefs occurs within countries, within schools and within classes than would be the case if self-confidence merely mirrored performance. That is to say, in any group of peers, even those with very low reading literacy levels, stronger performers are likely to have relatively high self-confidence, indicating that they base this on the norms they observe around them. This illustrates the importance of one's immediate environment in fostering the self-confidence that students need to develop as effective learners.

- Students reporting in PISA that they are good at verbal tasks do not necessarily also believe that they are good at mathematical tasks, despite the fact that in the PISA assessment there is an extremely high correlation between performance on these two scales. Indeed, in most countries there is at most a weak and in some cases a negative correlation between verbal and mathematical self-concept (see Table C3.3). This can again be explained by the fact that students' beliefs relate to subjective standards, observed relative to their own worlds. Thus, some students who are confident in reading may be less confident in mathematics partly because it is a relative weak point in relation to their own overall abilities and partly because they are more likely than weak readers to have peers who are good mathematicians.

Students' views of their ***verbal and mathematical abilities*** in different countries are shown in Figure 3.3. In this case, because students were asked whether they agreed or disagreed with statements, a distinction can be made between students who are positive overall and who are negative overall about themselves in these areas. The results show that confidence in verbal abilities is positive everywhere and also in every

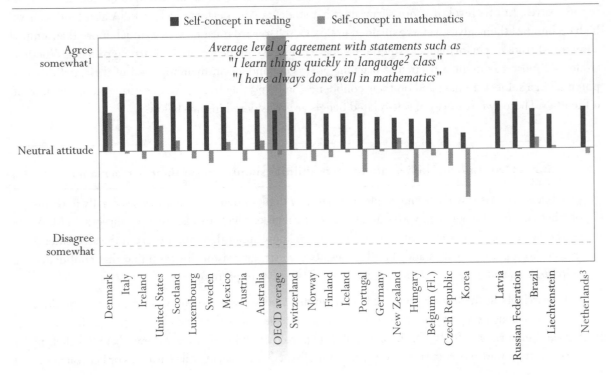

Figure 3.3

Student view of their verbal and mathematical abilities (self-concept)

■ Self-concept in reading   ■ Self-concept in mathematics

1. Scale has values of 1 "Disagree", 2 "Disagree somewhat", 3 "Agree somewhat" and 4 "Agree". A value of 2.5 is set as neutral attitude. All country mean stay between 2 "Disagree somewhat" and 3 "Agree somewhat".
2. Language of instruction in each country.
3. Response rate is too low to ensure comparability.
Source: OECD PISA Database, 2001. Table C3.2.

country stronger than confidence in mathematical abilities, which in most countries is negative overall. Thus more often than not, students have confidence in being able to cope with the challenges they are set in verbal tasks, but not in mathematics. More specifically:

• Danish students report greatest confidence in verbal ability, followed closely by students in Ireland, Italy, Scotland and the United States. This form of self-confidence is lowest in the Czech Republic and Korea.

• Danish students are also the most confident in mathematics and only they and students from the United States think about how well they do in mathematics in terms that are generally positive to a similar degree as occurs in all countries for verbal tasks. In contrast, students in Hungary, Korea and Portugal tend to have a particularly low view of how well they cope with mathematics.

• The gap between verbal and mathematical self-confidence is greatest in Hungary, Ireland, Italy and Korea.

Figure 3.4 looks at mean scores for *self-efficacy* – the degree to which students believe they can deal with learning challenges, even if they find them difficult. While the variation across countries here appears to be more modest than for students' beliefs about their specific abilities, Korean students again express the least self-confidence in this respect. On the other hand, the countries where students believe most in their efficacy are not the same as those where students have greatest confidence in particular abilities in verbal and mathematical tasks. Those in Austria, Brazil, Mexico and Sweden are most confident in being able to achieve even their difficult goals.

Figure 3.4

Student beliefs in their own efficacy

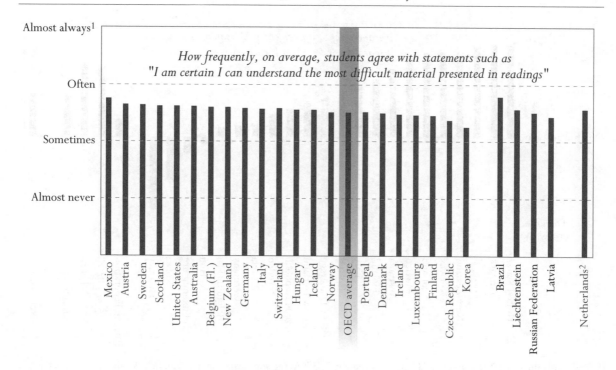

1. Scale ranges from 1 "Almost never" to 4 "Almost always".
2. Response rate is too low to ensure comparability.
Source: OECD PISA Database, 2001. Table C3.2.

Learning situation

Finally, PISA considered whether students like learning in competitive environments and whether they like learning in co-operative environments. It was possible to make valid cross-country comparisons only for *preferences for co-operative learning*. These are shown in Figure 3.5. While it is important to note that most differences in student preferences for learning situations occurs within rather between countries, the differences in the overall picture across countries produces notable results. Students in the United States, Denmark and Portugal on average score highly in this regard, indicating that they have had positive experiences with this form of learning and regard a team approach to (study) projects as beneficial. Students in Hungary and Korea are on average markedly negative towards this approach. In most countries, the attitude to co-operative learning is on balance positive. This is encouraging, showing that overall 15-year-old students today tend to enjoy working with other people and believe that this will help them produce good work.

Preference for co-operative and competitive forms of learning should not necessarily be regarded as being opposite or alternative student characteristics. In some countries, such as Korea, Latvia, Luxembourg and the Russian Federation, co-operative and competitive learning appear to be complementary motives, in the sense that students who have positive views about one are also more likely to be positive about the other. Interest in learning in either context is compatible with strong learning approaches. However, the extent to which students voice a preference for co-operative learning gives some indication of the approach they will take to co-operative projects in working life.

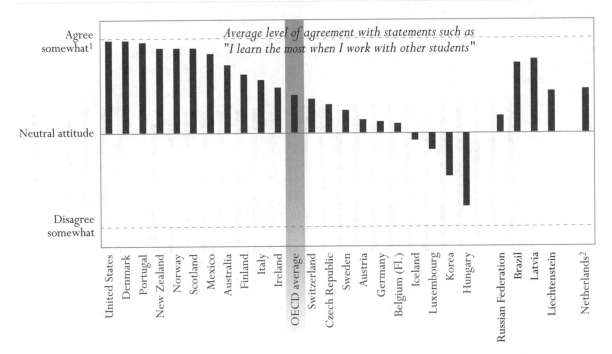

Figure 3.5

Student preference for co-operative learning

1. Scale has values of 1 " Disagree", 2 "Disagree somewhat", 3 " Agree somewhat" and 4 "Agree". A value of 2.5 is set as neutral attitude. All country mean stay between 2 "Disagree somewhat" and 3 "Agree somewhat".
2. Response rate is too low to ensure comparability.
Source: OECD PISA Database, 2001. Table C2.5g.

Clusters of students with similar characteristics

While it is not possible to compare the incidence of each individual student characteristic across countries, cluster analysis can be used to compare the patterns of such attributes across groups of students in each country. Specifically, this statistical technique can be used to characterise the degree to which students have different profiles, in terms of multiple characteristics that tend to go together. Chapter 2 has already shown that students who are, for example, better motivated also tend to use learning strategies more. But to what degree are such advantages and disadvantages concentrated among particular students? And how great are differences in performance among students with different sets of characteristics as learners?

Cluster analysis was applied to the results on the 13 scales of learner characteristics, standardised to express each student's scores relative to other students in the same country[2], thus eliminating cultural bias in terms of the different ways students describe their characteristics. The analysis divided all students in PISA into groups, aiming to maximise the degree to which those in the same group have similar characteristics and those in different groups have dissimilar characteristics. On this basis, it identified four student clusters of roughly equal size, whose characteristics are illustrated in Figure 3.6:

• Students in the first cluster are strong across the board in terms of their attitudes towards learning and learning behaviours. They can be characterised the ***strongest learners.***

• Students in the second cluster are stronger than average in these respects, except with respect to their interest and self-confidence in mathematics. They can be characterised as ***stronger learners, weaker in mathematics.***

- Students in the third cluster are weaker than average in most approaches to learning, but stronger in mathematics: ***weaker learners, stronger in mathematics.***

- Students in the final cluster are weak across the board, in their learning attitude and behaviours: the ***weakest learners.***

Figure 3.6

OECD mean scores in terms of student learning characteristics for the four student clusters

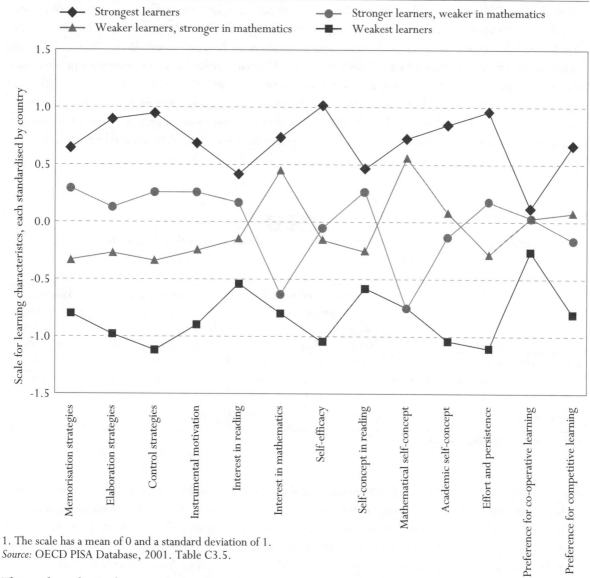

1. The scale has a mean of 0 and a standard deviation of 1.
Source: OECD PISA Database, 2001. Table C3.5.

This analysis shows that across countries:

- Strong self-confidence and interest in mathematics do not necessarily go with other strengths. The third cluster of students, with generally below-average learning strengths, are about as strong in these mathematics-related characteristics as the top group whose other characteristics are much stronger than the rest. Conversely, students in the second group, whose other characteristics are above average, only have mathematics-related attributes similar to the weakest learners overall.

• Some characteristics in each category are particularly likely to be strong among students with generally stronger approaches to learning and weak in the opposite case. Among learning strategies, stronger students are especially likely to use strategies employing comprehension: evaluation and control strategies. Such students are also likely to have especially high confidence in their ability to achieve even difficult goals (self-efficacy) and to put in a large amount of effort and persistence.

• Figure 3.7 shows that the 28 per cent of students classified as the strongest learners in terms of these characteristics overall have reading literacy performance 63 points or nearly one proficiency level higher than the one-fifth who come into the weakest learners category. In terms of mathematical performance, students with strong attitudes to mathematics but weaker in other characteristics (the third group) performed somewhat better in mathematics than those with the reverse profile in the second group. This shows the importance of particular mathematics-specific attitudes to mathematics performance. However, more general attitudes and learning behaviours are also closely associated with good performance in mathematics, as shown by a comparison in the mathematical literacy scores of clusters 2 and 4. These two groups have similar attitudes to mathematics, but those in cluster 2 have much stronger attributes in other respects and score on average 33 points higher on the mathematical literacy scale.

Figure 3.7

Performance on the combined reading literacy scale and the mathematical literacy scale for the students of the four clusters of learners

Cluster	Combined reading literacy scale			Mathematical literacy scale			Percentage of students in each cluster
	Mean score	S.E.	S.D.	Mean score	S.E.	S.D.	
1. Strongest learners	526	(3.4)	100	517	(4.0)	106	27.8
2. Stronger learners, weaker in mathematics	507	(2.7)	90	489	(3.1)	92	25.4
3. Weaker learners, stronger in mathematics	500	(2.9)	99	499	(3.3)	103	27.2
4. Weakest learners	463	(3.6)	96	456	(3.5)	96	19.6

Source: OECD PISA Database, 2001.

To what extent do these patterns vary across countries? Figure 3.8 shows how many students in each country fall into each cluster. Note that having a large number of students in the top cluster does *not* indicate that learner characteristics in a country are strong overall, since all of the scores are expressed relative to each country's norms. Rather it shows that relatively high scores in terms of different learner characteristics are relatively highly concentrated among certain students, rather than being distributed more evenly among different students. Overall, clustering patterns are similar in each country, but learning strengths are most highly concentrated in Finland, where 50 per cent of the students are characterised as either the strongest or the weakest learners and least in Belgium (Fl.) where 40 per cent in total come into these two categories. Another important feature of these results is the size of the group of students (weakest learners) who have not yet succeeded in acquiring the prerequisites for lifelong learning and are likely to need additional support to succeed. This group ranges from 17 per cent of the population in Austria, Belgium (Fl.), Germany, Italy, the Netherlands and Sweden to 22 per cent in Korea and the Russian Federation.

Figure 3.8

Percentage of students in each self-regulated learning cluster

■ Strongest learners   ■ Stronger learners, weaker in mathematics
■ Weaker learners, stronger in mathematics   ■ Weakest learners

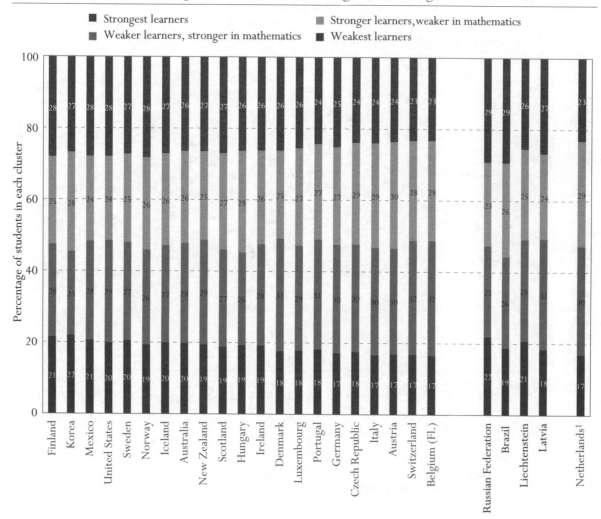

1. Response rate is too low to ensure comparability.
Source: OECD PISA Database, 2001. Table C3.6.

The general consistency of the relationship between learner characteristics and student performance is underlined by Figure 3.9, which shows the average reading literacy performance of students in each cluster, by country. The difference between the strongest and weakest learners of an average of about one proficiency level is fairly consistent across countries, although in Norway the gap is as high as 96 points and in Belgium (Fl.) it is 31 points. Note, however, that these differences range over very different levels of reading proficiency: in Finland the strongest learners are proficient on average near the top of Level 4, the weakest near the middle of Level 3; in Mexico the range is from the top of Level 1 to the top of Level 2.

There is not however a big gap in reading literacy performance between the middle two categories, whose characteristics on the non-mathematics related scales are somewhat above and somewhat below average respectively and in some countries this gap is non-existent. In some countries there is little difference between performance among the strongest learners and the second category of stronger learners: in fact,

Figure 3.9

Performance on the combined reading literacy scale for the four clusters of learners

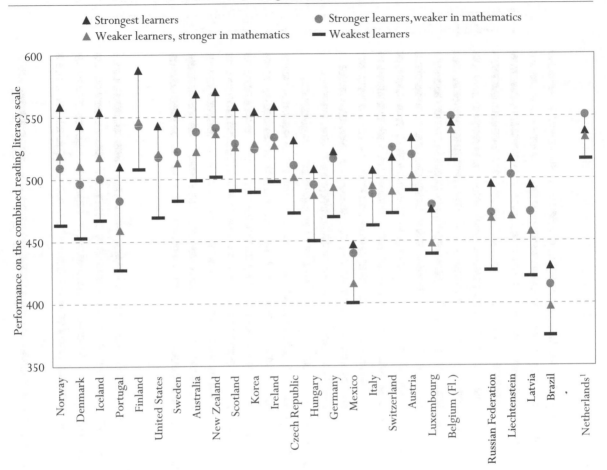

1. Response rate is too low to ensure comparability.
Source: OECD PISA Database, 2001. Table C3.6.

in Belgium (Fl.), Luxembourg and Switzerland, the latter category actually performs slightly better. These minor inconsistencies in the relationship between clusters of learner characteristics and performance reflect the fact that membership of a cluster does not measure student competence *per se*. In some cases, for example, better performing students may adopt less demanding strategies because they feel they have less need for them.

Countries, schools, students – where does the variation in learning approaches lie?

In reflecting on the above analysis on students' learning-related characteristics in the various countries participating in PISA, it is important to note that the differences *between* countries in students' reported characteristics are far less pronounced than the differences *within* countries. For the five characteristics for which student scores are directly comparable, the mean amount of variance that is explained between countries is 10 per cent or less, ranging from 10 per cent for memorisation strategies to 3 per cent for self-efficacy.

Moreover, there is also a very limited extent to which differences in learner characteristics within each country can be attributed to students having stronger characteristics in some schools than in others.

This is in contrast to school differences in student performance. Whereas 36 per cent of the variation in scores on the PISA literacy tests is between schools within countries (OECD, 2001), the mean variation in the measures of learning approaches that can be explained by school differences is just 7 per cent. This ranges from 0 per cent for instrumental motivation and self-concept in reading in Liechtenstein and mathematical self-concept in Luxembourg to 16 per cent for interest in mathematics in Latvia and Korea (see Table C3.4).

These results tell policy makers that in each country relatively few schools stand out as being particularly likely to have students who say they are well motivated, confident and use particular learning strategies. Such a result must be interpreted with some caution, given that they are based on self-reports and it is known that students' judgements about themselves can be strongly influenced by reference to their peers. In the case of some characteristics, this might disguise important between-school differences in students' true approaches to learning. For example, it is possible that some with hard-working classmates understate the amount of effort and persistence they put in, compared to students with less hard-working classmates, even though it is the absolute amount of effort that matters to school success. This makes it hard to identify schools with relatively hard-working pupils overall. On the other hand, in other respects, students' perceptions relative to their peers is an important part of the picture. For example even if some students' perception that they are not good at mathematics is linked to the high mathematics abilities of others in their school, rather an absolute weakness, this lack of confidence is still an important aspect of their approach to learning that may hold them back.

Thus the finding that individual schools do not vary greatly in the profile of students' self-reported approaches to learning has significant implications, even though it does not show that all schools are the same. What it does highlight is the great importance of variations in students as learners within each school. This underlines the need to focus attention on the effect that teachers can have on the weaker learners within each school and class. It is not sufficient to operate on the principle that "a rising tide raises all ships", since even in well-performing schools there are students who lack confidence and motivation and are not inclined to set and monitor their own learning goals.

Summary of key findings and their implications

The implications of the main findings in this chapter, which will be revisited in the policy discussion in Chapter 5, can be summarised as follows:

• Some education systems have managed to foster stronger characteristics in students as learners than others. Although this chapter has given only a limited range of comparisons, those that it provides suggest some clues about where policy might make a difference. For example, a general gap in student confidence in mathematics compared to reading has been contained more successfully in some countries than in others. Another interesting contrast is in the degree to which students have bought into the idea of co-operative learning. Such country differences indicate areas where some education systems could fruitfully work on improving the ways in which their students approach learning.

• The quarter of students with generally strong learner characteristics are reading at about one proficiency level above those with generally weak characteristics. This reinforces the importance of looking at the motivation, self-related beliefs and learning strategies that students use as a key aspect of improving performance.

• Students with stronger general learning approaches tend to have strong interest and self-confidence in reading, but less consistently so in mathematics. Some other students who are weaker overall have relatively positive approaches to mathematics and also perform well in mathematical literacy. This indicates both that approaches to mathematics can be a particular weakness that requires attention and that some students who like mathematics do well even in the absence of other strong characteristics as learners. In the latter case, mathematical interest and self-confidence may be a foundation on which other positive approaches to learning can built. The response by schools needs to involve co-ordination across the teaching force, to ensure that the various strengths and weaknesses of individuals are looked at together.

• In every school in every country, there is a wide range of learning approaches by different students. Thus, it cannot be assumed that schools with a good overall ethos, or with a socially advantaged intake, automatically create students who are all equally motivated, confident and well-equipped with learning strategies. Solutions need therefore to be sought, at the level of each class, particularly in terms of helping its weaker students to build confidence and motivation and to develop powerful learning strategies. It may be that certain general characteristics of education systems, such as teaching methods and the ability to work with families, need improving across the board in pursuit of these objectives.

Notes

1. See note 1 in Chapter 2 and Annex B.

2. Specifically, for each scale, student scores were adjusted so that in each country the mean score was equal to zero and the standard deviation equal to 1 *i.e.*, two-thirds of the student population in each country had scores between 1 and −1.

Chapter

4

DIFFERENCES IN THE APPROACHES TO LEARNING BETWEEN DIFFERENT GROUPS OF STUDENTS

KEY POINTS

- Male and female students tend to have distinctly different ways of approaching learning. Each has strengths and weaknesses. Male students tend to be more confident and interested in mathematics, are more likely to believe that they can overcome difficult learning challenges and enjoy competitive learning situations more. In some countries they are also more likely to use comprehension in processing new information (elaboration strategies). Female students tend to be more confident and interested in reading, think more about what they need to learn and put in more effort and persistence. In some countries they also use memorisation more and are more favourable than males to learning co-operatively.

- Students from more privileged social backgrounds have some clear advantages in the way they approach learning. The most consistent and evident advantage in most countries (although to quite different degrees) is their greater self-confidence, along with a higher interest in reading and a greater propensity to control their own learning. However, socially disadvantaged students are in most countries no less likely to say they try hard, to be motivated by the external rewards of learning such as getting a good job, or to memorise information. In a number of countries they are more likely than advantaged students to enjoy learning in co-operative situations.

- Although immigrant students come on average from less advantaged social backgrounds and show lower performance on the PISA assessments, they tend to have no weaker and in some respects stronger approaches to learning than native-born students. This is most clearly true in certain countries, particularly Australia, New Zealand and Sweden, where immigrant students are stronger in a majority of the learner characteristics measured in PISA. Across countries, immigrant students' greatest relative strengths are in interest in mathematics and competitive learning. However, overall the differences between immigrant and native-born students tend to be relatively small.

- Students who have the highest reading literacy show much stronger learning approaches than weaker readers in all countries. In particular, they have stronger beliefs in their own abilities, greater interest in reading and are more likely to control their learning. Weaker readers are at least as likely to enjoy co-operative learning as stronger ones.

Introduction

The last two chapters have noted that learning strengths and weaknesses tend to be concentrated among certain groups of students. A student who is poorly motivated, for example, is also likely to lack self-confidence and make limited use of learning strategies. This implies that policies to improve approaches to learning need particularly to focus on groups of students facing multiple limitations. To what extent are certain groups within the population at risk of having weak approaches to learning? And are some groups particular weak on certain characteristics? The answers can help policy-makers to develop targeted responses.

This chapter considers the learning approaches of three groups defined by their background characteristics – by gender, socio-economic background and immigrant status. It then considers a fourth group defined by learning outcomes: students with low reading literacy. The identification in Chapter 2 of associations between approaches to learning and performance has already told us that these low achievers have weaker characteristics as learners, but a focus on them as a group helps to pinpoint which of these traits require closest attention.

Gender differences in approaches to learning

All countries recognise the paramount importance of reducing educational disparities between male and female students. Past efforts to combat disadvantages experienced by females, related in particular to career pathways, have contributed to a reduction in gender gaps for example in mathematics and science achievement. More recently, countries have started to focus on problems of low-achieving males, especially in relation to reading. PISA 2000 showed females ahead of males in reading literacy in every country, by an average of 32 points or nearly half a proficiency level. Males are ahead in mathematics literacy in half the countries, but by a smaller amount – an average of 11 points; in the other half there was no significant gender difference (OECD, 2001).

Do these performance differences reflect strengths and weaknesses of each sex in their approaches to learning? The results, summarised in Figure 4.1, show not a clear advantage for either males or females, but rather suggest that each has distinctive strengths and weaknesses in the way they approach learning.

Box D. A standardised way of measuring differences between groups: Effect sizes

This chapter shows the magnitude of differences between groups in terms that allow them to be compared on a common basis for different characteristics in different countries. An effect size measures the difference between, say, the interest in reading of male and female students in Germany, relative to the average variation in interest in reading scores among German male and among German female students. An effect size of 1 would mean that the average male and female reading interest differs by one standard deviation, indicating a big difference. As a measure of dispersion, a standard deviation (S.D.) indicates the range within which the scores of a certain proportion of the population are located: roughly two-thirds have scores between one standard deviation above the mean and one standard deviation below the mean.

The following is a recognised interpretation of the amount of difference signified by various effect sizes: small: $d \leq 0.20$; medium $d = 0.50$; large ≥ 0.80.

See also Annex D for fuller explanation.

Figure 4.1
Summary of gender differences in learner characteristics

Characteristics	In how many of 21 OECD countries[1] is there a significant male-female difference?	OECD average effect size
		Female advantage
Interest in reading	Female advantage in all countries but Korea	0.53
Self-concept in reading	Female advantage in 18 countries	0.29
Control strategies	Female advantage in 16 countries	0.18
Effort and persistence	Female advantage in 14 countries	0.16
Preference for co-operative learning	Female advantage in 11 countries; male in Korea	0.10
Memorisation strategies	Female advantage in 10 countries; male in Norway	0.10
Academic self-concept	Female advantage in Italy; male in Denmark	0.02
		Male advantage
Elaboration strategies	Male advantage in 7 countries	0.06
Interest in mathematics	Male advantage in 14 countries	0.20
Preference for competitive learning	Male advantage in 16 countries	0.21
Self-efficacy	Male advantage in 18 countries	0.22
Mathematical self-concept	Male advantage in 17 countries	0.25

1. Excludes the Netherlands, for which the response rate is too low to ensure comparability.
Source: OECD PISA Database, 2001. Table C4.1.

The biggest single difference between male and female students shown in the figure is that the latter are more likely to be interested in reading: this effect of 0.5 is of medium size. In five other respects there are smaller but still distinct gender differences of between 0.2 and 0.3, four of them to the advantage of males.

Interestingly, in each of the four categories of student characteristics, described in Figure 1.1, males have stronger features in some respects and females in others:

• Some *learning strategies* are more commonly applied by females: most notably, they are more likely than males to control their learning in all but four OECD countries. Yet when it comes to the other comprehension-oriented strategy, elaboration, the only cases where there are significant differences favour males, though in no case is the difference great. Thus while females are generally better at working out what they need to know, this advantage does not extend to information processing skills.

• *Motivation* shows contrasting gender differences. In most countries girls express significantly greater reading interest and claim more effort and persistence. On the other hand, boys show significantly more interest in mathematics in most countries – by small degrees in some countries, but by much more in others (*e.g.,* Switzerland, where the effect size is 0.51).

• Students' *self-related beliefs* show similar patterns, with females generally confident in their verbal abilities and males in their mathematical abilities. A particular advantage for male students, their biggest strength outside the mathematics domain, is their confidence in being able to succeed in tasks, even where they find them difficult. Even though the extent of this advantage is modest, its incidence is widespread: it is identifiable at a statistically significant level in all but three OECD countries.

- Males and females have different *learning preferences*: in most countries males are more likely than females to be positive about competitive learning situations. In about half of countries, females are more likely than males to say that they like learning co-operatively; in the rest there is no difference, except in Korea where males favour co-operative learning more.

Such gender differences vary considerably from one country to another. Figure 4.2a summarises some key features of each country's gender differences, looking at selected features that particularly distinguish males' and females' motivation, self-related beliefs and use of learning strategies and setting these alongside the difference between males and females in reading literacy performance: the countries are ranked by how far ahead females are in reading. This shows no systematic relationship between the differences between male and female learning approaches and differences in their performance, but some varying country profiles. For example, Denmark, Finland, Norway and Sweden are all countries where male students have considerably greater confidence than females in their efficacy as learners and where females are little or no more likely (and in Norway males are more likely) to control their learning. Yet in Finland, where females are much more interested in reading than males, they are also further ahead in reading literacy than in any other country, whereas in Denmark, where the gap in reading interest is closer to average, the performance gap is much smaller.

Across all 13 characteristics shown in Figure 4.1, several other country contrasts stand out:

- In Belgium (Fl.) and in Luxembourg, there are significant differences between males and females in 11 characteristics; in Korea, only in two.

- Females are ahead in the most aspects in the Czech Republic, Luxembourg and the Russian Federation (on 7 characteristics); in Korea they are ahead in no respects and in Liechtenstein and Sweden only in two.

- Males are ahead in the most aspects in Denmark, the Netherlands and Norway (on 7 characteristics); in the United States they are ahead in no aspect and in Hungary, Latvia, Mexico and the Russian Federation only in one.

Where do males and females fall in the clusters described in Chapter 3?

Chapter 3 divided students into four clusters according to their overall characteristics as learners – one with strong characteristics across the board, the second with above average characteristics except relating to mathematics, a third with below average characteristics except in mathematics and the fourth with generally weak characteristics.

Despite the fact that both male and female students have strengths and weaknesses as learners, a striking result is that considerably more males than females are in the cluster with the strongest characteristics (33 per cent of males, 24 per cent of females), with the reverse true of the second category in which students are above average except in their confidence and interest in mathematics (21 per cent of males, 32 per cent of females). In Germany, Liechtenstein, the Netherlands and Switzerland, these gender differences exceed 15 percentage points.

It is difficult to interpret this apparent male advantage in terms of clustered characteristics, since so many factors interact to define the clusters. However, one possible explanation would be that among students with generally strong characteristics, limitations in attitudes towards mathematics are more likely to show among females than are limitations in attitudes towards reading in the case of males.

In the bottom two clusters, males and females are about equally represented.

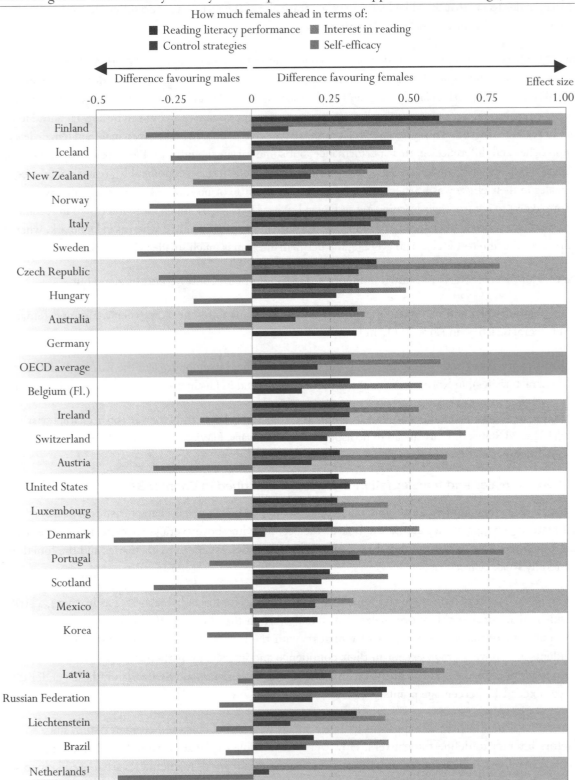

Figure 4.2a

Selected gender differences by country: student performance and approaches to learning (effect sizes)

How much females ahead in terms of:
■ Reading literacy performance   ■ Interest in reading
■ Control strategies   ■ Self-efficacy

1. Response rate is too low to ensure comparability.
Source: OECD PISA Database, 2001. Tables C3.1b and C4.1.

Are the relationships to performance described in Chapter 2 the same for males and females?

Any policy response to gender differences needs to consider the degree to which, within each country, various characteristics are associated with performance. For example, does a lack of interest in reading appear to hold back males to the same degree as females? In fact, the strength of these effects, presented for all students in Chapter 2, are mainly of equal strength for both sexes. Only in a minority of cases do correlation coefficients differ by more than 0.1 and in virtually no case[1] by more than 0.2. These represent relatively small, though not insignificant, differences in the strength of association.

Such gender differences in the strength of the association between learner characteristics and performance tend to show stronger effects for the gender whose average strength in the relevant characteristic is greater (Figure 4.2b). Thus for example females have greater reading interest and within half of countries, more interest in reading makes a notably greater[2] difference to predicted performance for females than for males. In other countries there is no difference. Conversely, in seven out of eight countries where with gender differences in the strength of association between self-efficacy and performance, it is stronger for males, who tend to have greater beliefs in self-efficacy overall. These results indicate that there may in some cases be a greater payoff in improving a student's weaknesses in attributes in which other students of their own sex tend to be strong (*e.g.,* low reading interest for a female), than in improving weaknesses that are shared with others of one's sex (*e.g.,* low reading interest for males). However, a more general response in the opposite direction – of giving each gender particular help and encouragement in areas where they are generally weak – is not contradicted by these findings: first, because the differences in

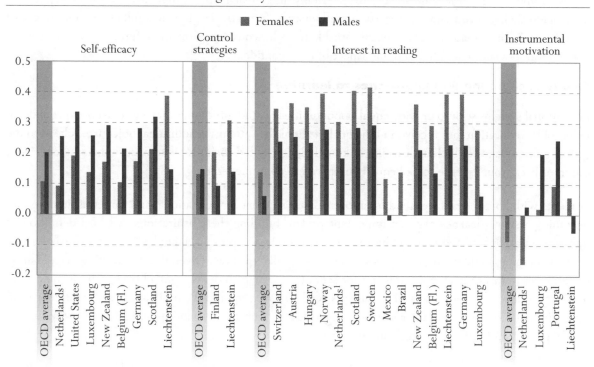

Figure 4.2b

Most notable gender differences in the relationships
between reading literacy and selected learner characteristics

1. Response rate is too low to ensure comparability.
Source: OECD PISA Database, 2001. Table C4.1.

association with performance are relatively small and second because positive approaches to learning are desirable outcomes in their own right.

Implications of gender differences

The above results show important differences between males and females as learners, with significant differences on most of the 13 measured characteristics in all but four countries. This shows that just as countries have undertaken initiatives to address gender inequalities in performance, so there is a need to give gender-specific help to students in improving their characteristics as learners.

In general, female students in most countries adopt a more self-evaluating perspective during the learning process, making more use of control strategies. However, they could be helped by training in the use of strategies that lead to a deeper understanding of material (elaboration). Males are already better at relating new and previously acquired material, but could be helped to plan, structure and monitor their learning independently.

The results also show that schools and societies, do not always succeed in fostering comparable levels of motivation, interest or self-confidence in different areas among male and female students, with knock-on implications for performance. Male students need to be helped towards a more positive approach to reading, which requires them to see it as a useful, profitable and enjoyable activity. Teachers need to consider the expectations that they have of students of both sexes and adopt strategies to raise the levels of self-confidence and motivation of students in those areas where each are weak.

This cannot be achieved simply through classroom practice, since reading is a cultural practice influenced by the social context. Hurrelmann (1994) emphasises the need to provide children and adolescents with a motivating reading environment and reading role models. Promoting male reading interest therefore needs to involve the family and society more widely. In similar respects, females need wide support in developing their interest and self-regard in mathematics. In particular, female students who do not have confidence in their mathematical abilities are likely to be constrained in their future choice of career, making it important to aim to build this aspect of their confidence.

Family background and approaches to learning

Educational systems seek to provide equal opportunities to students from differing social backgrounds, in terms of the education they receive and the qualifications they attain. An additional objective, related to the growing importance of lifelong learning in knowledge-oriented societies, is to ensure that students from different backgrounds leave school equally prepared to continue learning.

Students with home advantages tend to enjoy stronger support for educational and career aspirations and becoming a strong learner plays an important part in fulfilling these aspirations. A broad definition of human capital, formulated recently by the OECD (2002c, Chapter 5), includes "the characteristics that allow a person to build, manage and deploy his or her skills" (p. 118). Given the strong influence of family experiences in this respect, a key mission for schools is to help students from all backgrounds to develop learning *capacity*. The degree to which students aged 15 have acquired the motivation, self-confidence and strategies needed to regulate their learning, regardless of their background, is an indicator of the success of school systems in producing such an outcome.

Social background is here measured by socio-economic status, according to parental occupation. In PISA occupations were coded in accordance with the International Standard Classification of Occupations

(ISCO-88), ranked on an index that disentangles the socio-economic status of an occupation from its prestige (Ganzeboom *et al*, 1992). Students' scores on this index, the PISA International Socio-Economic Index of Occupational Status (ISEI), were assigned according to the occupational status of their mother or father, whichever is higher (HISEI).

To measure differences by student background, the following analysis compares the characteristics of students in two groups: the top quarter and the bottom national quarter of the student population in each country, when ranked by their parent's occupational status scores (HISEI). Note that each of these groups does not represent students with an identical social profile in each country. The higher group have average socio-economic status ranging from 79 in the Russian Federation to 63 in Korea, on a 90-point index. The lower group's scores range from 24 in Mexico to 35 in Norway. The gap between the groups ranges from 46 in Latvia to 35 in the Czech Republic (see Table C4.5). Thus the comparisons presented below show differences in student characteristics relative to social differences as they are distributed within each country rather than relative to an internationally standard amount of social difference.

Figure 4.3 summarises the difference between these two groups in terms of the 13 learner characteristics measured in PISA. As with the gender comparisons, it uses a standardised measure, effect sizes (see Box D), to compare the degree to which students with parents from high and low economic status differ on each characteristic, relative to overall student differences in this characteristic. The results show significant social disparities, but stronger with respect to some characteristics than others:

• In terms of learning strategies, students from higher socio-economic groups make more use of control and elaboration strategies in most countries, but there is no clear social pattern in the use of memorisation.

Figure 4.3

Summary of learner characteristics by social background: Difference between top and bottom quarters of students ranked by socio-economic status

Characteristics	In how many of 21 OECD countries[1] is the top quarter of students significantly different from the bottom quarter ?	OECD average effect size
Self-efficacy	Top quarter stronger in all but Belgium (Fl.)	0.40
Academic self-concept	Top quarter stronger in 17 countries	0.32
Self-concept in reading	Top quarter stronger in 18 countries	0.28
Control strategies	Top quarter stronger in 18 countries	0.26
Interest in reading	Top quarter stronger in 19 countries	0.26
Elaboration strategies	Top quarter stronger in 13 countries	0.22
Mathematical self-concept	Top quarter stronger in 13 countries	0.21
Preference for competitive learning	Top quarter stronger in 12 countries; Bottom quarter in Switzerland	0.16
Effort and persistence	Top quarter stronger in 8 countries	0.14
Interest in mathematics	Top quarter stronger in 8 countries; Bottom quarter stronger in 2 countries	0.10
Instrumental motivation	Top quarter stronger in 5 countries; Bottom quarter stronger in 2 countries	0.06
Memorisation	Top quarter stronger in 3 countries; Bottom quarter stronger in 6 countries	-0.01
Preference for co-operative learning	Bottom quarter stronger in 10 countries	-0.13

1. Excludes the Netherlands, for which the response rate is too low to ensure comparability.
Source: OECD PISA Database, 2001. Table C4.2.

• In terms of motivation, students with higher socio-economic status in most countries show greater interest in reading, but in other respects the pattern is less clear-cut. They show greater interest in mathematics and greater effort and persistence to a significant degree in just over a third of countries and greater instrumental motivation only in a quarter. In Austria and Switzerland, students from *lower* socio-economic groups show greater interest in mathematics and in Austria and Belgium (Fl.) they are more likely than those in higher groups to be motivated by external factors such as job prospects.

• The self-related beliefs of students whose parents have higher-status jobs are much more consistently above those with lower socio-economic status. In particular, the former are more likely to believe in their capacity to tackle learning challenges (self-efficacy) in every OECD country except Belgium (Fl.). In Denmark, Iceland, Norway and Sweden the effect is over 0.5, indicating medium to high differences. Students' confidence in their ability to perform verbal, mathematical and general academic tasks is also stronger for those with higher socio-economic status in the majority of countries. The social gap in academic self-concept is especially strong in three countries: Norway (effect size of 0.71), Finland (effect size of 0.54) and Sweden (effect size of 0.51). Thus it is these forms of self-confidence that distinguish students of different social backgrounds most consistently among the factors examined here and in the Nordic countries this effect appears to be particularly important.

• In terms of learning preferences, students in about half of countries are more likely to show enthusiasm for competitive learning if they have high socio-economic status; only in Switzerland is the reverse true. The effect is low on average but exceeds 0.3 in Australia, Iceland and Norway. On the other hand, where there is a difference in attitudes to co-operative learning, again in about half of countries, it is those from lower socio-economic backgrounds who favour it more. The differences however are all small (below 0.25).

Figure 4.4 shows some differences in the learning approaches of students from different backgrounds, looking at key features that particularly distinguish their levels of self-confidence, motivation and use of learning strategies. It only shows effect sizes greater than 0.3, which exist for at least one of the characteristics shown in every country except Brazil, Italy and Liechtenstein.

Overall, the countries with significant social differences in the greatest number of the 13 characteristics are Sweden (with all 13), Finland (with 12), Korea, Norway and the Russian Federation (all with 11). It is particularly striking to note that all of the Nordic countries have relatively strong social differences in approaches to learning, especially in students' self-esteem, despite the fact that these countries also have low social disparities in terms of student performance (OECD, 2001). This illustrates an important point: that even where school systems manage to enable students from disadvantaged backgrounds to perform relatively well at school, it can be harder to change certain underlying self-beliefs. These can have knock-on effects for students in later life. Research suggests that those from disadvantaged backgrounds who perform well tend to be more cautious in decisions about career development and in choices about higher education than more advantaged students with the same school performance.

Implications of socio-economic differences

The above results show that different approaches to learning give students from more favourable socio-economic backgrounds important advantages, but that these differences are not consistent across the board.

Figure 4.4

Selected differences between students from different socio-economic backgrounds

Graph shows effect sizes above 0.30 in:

■ Self-efficacy
■ Control strategies
■ Interest in reading

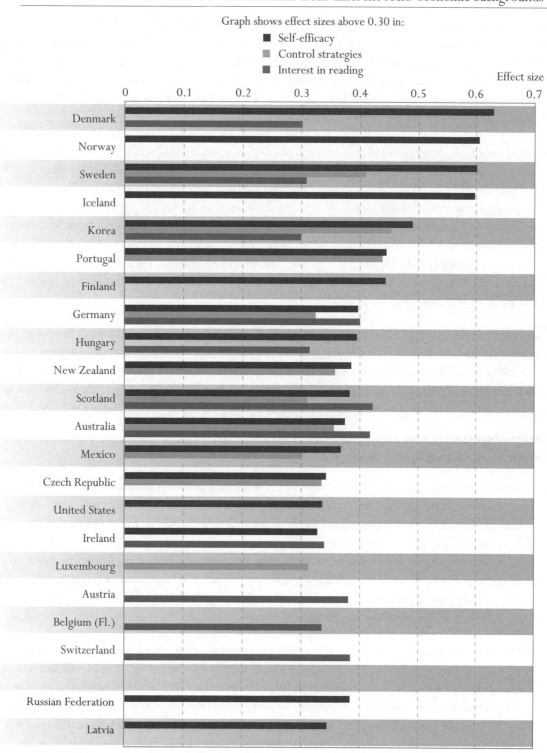

Source: OECD PISA Database, 2001. Table C4.2.

This has implications for where schools focus their attention in addressing social inequalities in student approaches to learning:

• Socially disadvantaged students do not have an obvious disadvantage in terms of the extent to which they learn material through memory, but in general are much less likely to adopt comprehension-oriented strategies involving the combining of new and existing knowledge and conscious checking of what they still need to learn against their learning goals. This suggests that such students need particular help in employing these more sophisticated learning strategies. Teachers in turn may require better training in how to encourage such habits among less advantaged students.

• In most countries, disadvantaged students appear to put in just as much effort as their advantaged peers and are at least as likely by age 15 to see the point of studying to get a good job. Where their motivation falls most clearly short, however, is in their intrinsic interest in reading. This may well be a result of less stimulating home environments, with fewer resources such as books. Engagement in reading has been shown to be of crucial importance in overcoming social disadvantage: students from less advantaged families who read a lot and enjoy it tend to outperform those with more home advantages but less reading engagement (OECD, 2002b; Guthrie and Wigfield, 2000). Thus it is essential for schools systems and individual teachers to focus on developing and maintaining an interest in reading among disadvantaged students.

• Students from disadvantaged backgrounds tend to lack confidence in their own abilities in a range of ways. Compared with their peers, they believe less strongly in their competence in particular subjects as well as in their ability to face learning challenges that they find difficult. This shows that schools have had limited success in counteracting the influence of family environment on some students' view of themselves as learners. However, some countries have succeeded more than others (see Figure 4.4 and Table C4.2).

Immigration status and approaches to learning: Differences between students with and without an immigrant background

As migration becomes more common, it affects the lives of a growing number of students. Immigrant children of school-going age face the challenge of adapting to a new environment, to a new school and to a new education system. Often they also have to adapt to a new language. In 12 out of the 14 countries in PISA where at least 3 per cent of students and their parents were born abroad, the majority of these students speak a language at home that is not that of the country where they are living. This contrasts with under 3 per cent of native students, speaking a different language in the home, in all but two countries. Moreover, in almost all of the countries, immigrant students have lower socio-economic status on average than native-born students, with the largest gaps in Austria, Germany, Luxembourg and Switzerland.

In light of these disadvantages, it is not surprising that immigrant students in PISA show lower average levels of reading literacy than native students: in 10 out of 15 countries with significant immigrant populations, the gap exceeds one proficiency level (OECD, 2001). But do they have weaker approaches to learning? The following analysis considers this by comparing characteristics of immigrant students who, as well as their parents, were born outside the country where they go to school, with native students who, as well as at least one parent, were born in that country. It only looks at the 14 countries in the survey where at least 3 per cent of students are immigrants.

Figure 4.5

Figure 4.5
Summary of main differences in learner characteristics by immigrant status

Characteristics (showing only those for which differences exist in at least 5 OECD countries)	In how many of 11 OECD countries[1] where at least 3 per cent of students are immigrants were there significant differences between immigrants and native students?	Average effect size in these 11 countries (immigrant student advantage)
Interest in mathematics	Immigrants stronger in 8 countries	0.32
Preference for competitive learning	Immigrants stronger in 6 countries	0.25
Memorisation strategies	Immigrants stronger in 5 countries	0.23
Instrumental motivation	Immigrants stronger in 5 countries	0.16
Self-concept in reading	Immigrants stronger in Sweden; Native students in 3 countries	-0.18

1. Excludes the Netherlands, for which the response rate is too low to ensure comparability.
Source: OECD PISA Database, 2001. Table C4.3.

The results, summarised in Figure 4.5, do not in fact show that immigrant students are weaker in their approaches to learning. Rather, they show fewer significant differences than for the other sub-groups of students considered in this chapter and those differences that do exist mostly show migrant students with stronger characteristics than native ones. In particular, they have stronger interest in mathematics and a greater inclination for competitive learning in at least half of the countries shown. On the other hand, there is not a single country with significant differences between native and immigrant students in their interest in reading.

However, the most distinctive patterns in this case concern not characteristics where differences are most frequent across countries, but particular countries with more frequent differences across a range of learner characteristics. This may reflect the fact that the composition and situation of immigrant groups in different countries varies considerably. As shown in Figure 4.6, immigrant students in Australia and New Zealand have stronger approaches than native students across nine or ten of the 13 student attributes measured. In Denmark, no significant differences in learning approaches were identified. Only in Latvia were native students stronger in several respects – interest in mathematics, academic self-concept, preference for competitive learning and co-operative learning.

Most of the observed differences were small to moderate in size, with effect sizes mainly between 0.2 and 0.4.

Since immigrant students thus sometimes show stronger approaches to learning despite their lower socio-economic status, it is worth considering what the differences are if one controls for this factor – *i.e.,* when comparing immigrant and native students with similar social backgrounds. In these terms, there are almost no cases where native students have stronger learning characteristics (the only statistically significant case is Germany for preference for co-operative learning). Controlling for social background also would increase the number of incidents[3] where immigrant students have significantly stronger learning characteristics than native students.

Implications of differences between immigrant and native students

The results above do not produce a general pattern, but may rather reflect the specific characteristics of countries and of certain learner characteristics. Nevertheless, it is notable that despite their underperformance in the PISA assessment, immigrant students are more often stronger than native students in terms of motivation, self-confidence and learning strategies. In two countries, Australia and New Zealand, they show particular strengths across these categories; in Australia's case this result is

Figure 4.6

Number of learning characteristics for which immigrant students are significantly different from native students

- ■ Immigrant students stronger
- □ No significant difference
- ■ Native students stronger

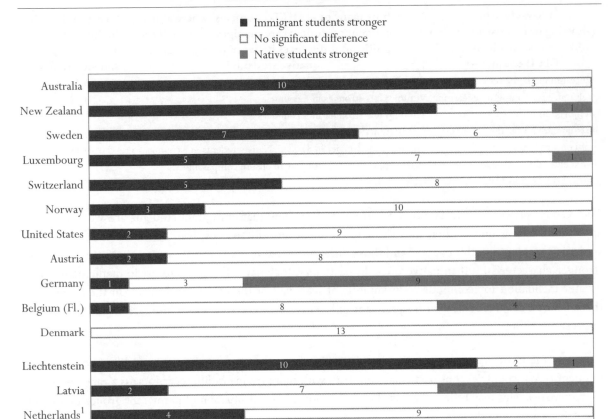

1. Response rate is too low to ensure comparability.
Source: OECD PISA Database, 2001. Table C4.3.

consistent with the fact that students from immigrant families are not outperformed by native students in reading, mathematics and science literacy.

One question that arises is why immigrant students, who often speak a minority language in the home and who are on average weaker readers than native students, nevertheless show an interest in reading that is not significantly different from that of their peers. An explanation may be that this interest, as well as their confidence in their verbal abilities, is not based solely on reading the language spoken at school. Immigrant students' marked interest in mathematics may arise because for those who speak another language at home, mathematics instruction represents a welcome alternative to subjects focusing more strongly on verbal components.

Another telling result is the greater instrumental motivation shown by immigrant students in many countries. This may reflect the desire for upward economic social mobility among families trying to get established in a new society.

It should be emphasised that PISA has found limited scope for differentiating results on the basis of immigrant status, partly because immigrant populations as a whole are often so heterogeneous. Yet it is encouraging that, unlike in the case of performance, there appears to be no overall disadvantage suffered by immigrant groups when it comes to learning approaches. This argues well for the future of such groups as lifelong learners and indicates that there is no systematic discrimination that harms the prospects of immigrant students in acquiring positive approaches to learning.

Differences between the learning approaches of weak and strong readers

Chapter 2 has already demonstrated that there are strong links between approaches to learning and performance in reading. Looking at strong and weak readers as contrasting sub-groups is likely to confirm these results. However, it can also add detail to the picture by considering specifically the learning profile of weak and strong readers, in terms of the characteristics in which they particularly excel of fall short.

Figure 4.7 and Figure 4.8 summarise the difference between the quarter of students with the highest PISA reading literacy scores in each country (strong readers) and those with the lowest (weak readers). Note that by this definition a weak reader in one country can have a very different average reading literacy score from a weak reader in another: strength and weakness are here measured in relation to one's fellow-nationals. These results show that in several respects, differences in approaches to learning between strong and weak readers are consistently high, but in others the difference is less marked:

- In terms of learning strategies, the pattern is similar to that of students from different social backgrounds. Stronger readers are more likely to use control strategies and elaboration strategies than weaker readers, but there is no consistent difference in their use of memorisation. Note that control strategies are used more by strong readers in every country and although the relationship is particularly strong (effect size above 0.8) only in the Czech Republic and Portugal, there is a medium to strong effect of between 0.50 and 0.80 in a further 11 OECD countries.

Figure 4.7

Summary of differences in learner characteristics between strong and weak readers

Characteristics	In how many of 21 OECD countries[1] is there a significant difference in learning approaches between strong and weak readers?	OECD average effect size
Interest in reading	Strong readers more in all except Mexico	0.80
Academic self-concept	Strong readers more in all 21 countries	0.74
Self-concept in reading	Strong readers more in all 21 countries	0.69
Self-efficacy	Strong readers more in all 21 countries	0.61
Control strategies	Strong readers more in all 21 countries	0.52
Effort and persistence	Strong readers more in 19 countries	0.37
Mathematical self-concept	Strong readers more in 17 countries	0.37
Elaboration strategies	Strong readers more in 18 countries	0.33
Preference for competitive learning	Strong readers more in 16 countries; Weak readers more in Portugal	0.23
Instrumental motivation	Strong readers more in 10 countries; Weak readers more in Italy	0.19
Interest in mathematics	Strong readers more in 6 countries; Weak readers more in 2 countries	0.10
Memorisation strategies	Strong readers more in 6 countries; Weak readers more in 4 countries	0.02
Preference for co-operative learning	Weak readers more in 5 countries	-0.09

1. Excludes the Netherlands, for which the response rate is too low to ensure comparability.
Source: OECD PISA Database, 2001. Table C4.4.

Figure 4.8
Countries with the largest differences in learning approaches between strong and weak readers

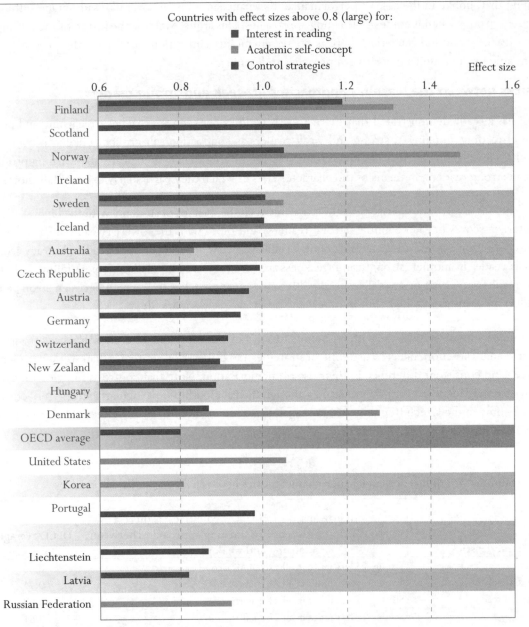

Source: OECD PISA Database, 2001. Tables C4.8a and C4.8b.

- In terms of motivation, easily the biggest difference between strong and weak readers in most countries is in their interest in reading. Of all the differences in learning approaches between groups of students considered in this chapter, the tendency for stronger readers to be more positive about reading is the greatest, with an effect size of 0.8, rated as large, on average in OECD countries. Better readers are also more likely to put in more effort in most countries, although the size of this effect is on average only half as great as for interest in reading. In about half of countries, stronger readers are more likely than weaker readers to be motivated by external factors like job prospects, but this effect is generally small and in Italy the reverse is true.

- The self-related beliefs of stronger readers are consistently higher than those of weaker ones. For all four measures in this category, the effect size is at least medium (above 0.5) and in Denmark, Finland, Iceland and Norway it is close to three times this strength for academic self-concept. In general, students who do not read well are highly unlikely to think much of their academic abilities and this negative view of themselves is likely to hold back their progress as learners.

The learning preferences of strong and weak readers can differ: in most countries stronger ones are more likely to feel more positive than weaker ones about competitive learning. The opposite is true, on average, for preference for co-operative learning, but there is no significant difference in most countries. In Australia, Belgium (Fl.), Denmark, Hungary and Sweden, weak readers have a significantly higher preference for co-operative learning than stronger ones. Does this mean that students with a disposition for working in groups do not manage to achieve as much as those with a more individualistic streak, or conversely that students who are weak in reading may gain strength from an ability to engage in group learning situations? These data on their own cannot answer this question, but at least raise the possibility that the latter is true. Since it is essential to find areas where weak readers can be engaged, this merits further investigation.

Implications of differences between strong and weak readers

Weak readers in all countries encounter severe difficulties in developing effective learning strategies, in their motivation and in their self-confidence. Yet the ability to become competent and self-driven learners is vital if they are to take advantage of further educational, training and other learning activities after leaving school, since independent learning is a precondition for many opportunities in work and post-school education.

The evidence indicates that specific attention is needed to improve weak readers' interest in reading and their self-confidence, both of which are particularly likely to be low. Reading interest is a feature of engagement that has already been shown (OECD, 2002*b*) to be vital in relation to performance at school, but is also likely to be important in sustaining learning interest in later life. Self-related beliefs are inevitably weaker for students who perform poorly at school, but longitudinal evidence (Bandura, 1994) has shown that greater self-confidence can also be a stepping-stone to better performance. Moreover, if students reach 15 with a low view of their effectiveness as learners, they are less likely to take on learning challenges in adulthood. In general, teachers need much stronger training in techniques that allow them to build weaker students' confidence and motivation at the same time as demonstrating to them the value of using particular learning strategies. They cannot tackle these tasks alone and need to work with others including families, but teachers can play a pivotal role in this respect.

One potentially positive sign from this analysis is the relatively favourable view that weaker readers have of co-operative learning: in all countries they like it at least as much as stronger readers and in some countries more. While further investigation is needed before concluding that this indicates strength of co-operative learning as an approach for weak readers, rather than a weakness of those who engage in it, it would be unwise for education systems to neglect such a potential avenue for engaging students who urgently need to become more positive about learning.

Notes

1. The sole exception is for self-efficacy in Liechtenstein.

2. Correlation coefficients differ by at least 0.1.

3. An "incident" means a particular student characteristic (*i.e.*, memorisation strategies, elaboration strategies) in a particular country where immigrant students are statistically significantly stronger than native students. These are presented in Table C4.3 and the results are based on comparisons of immigrants and native students without taking into consideration of their socio-economic status of their parents.

KEY FINDINGS AND POLICY
IMPLICATIONS

Introduction

Positive student approaches to learning are both necessary for success in schools and important as outcomes of schooling in their own right. In particular, students need the motivation, self-confidence and learning strategies that allow them to drive and regulate their own learning activity. This report has analysed the degree to which students in different countries and particular groups of students within countries, have acquired characteristics as learners that are essential for life-long learning and success in future life. The degree to which students' capacities to regulate their own learning affect their school achievement has also

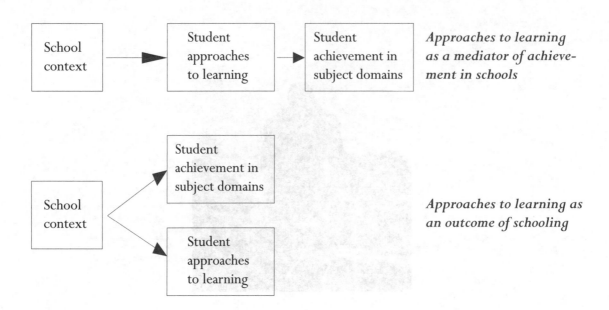

been analysed by exploring the relationships between these characteristics and performance in the PISA reading literacy tests.

Introduction to key results of the cross-national analysis of student approaches to learning

The analysis has produced measures relating to both types of outcome shown in the above diagram. It has also shed important light on the relationship between different aspects of student approaches to learning and thus on the whole process that makes students into competent autonomous learners. These findings are now summarised in turn.

a) Predicting performance

The first rationale behind efforts to improve students' approaches to learning is that these forms of learning have a positive effect on student performance. Students who can regulate their own learning in an effective manner are assumed to set realistic goals, to select learning strategies and techniques appropriate to the demands of the task at hand, to shield themselves from competing intentions and to maintain motivation when learning.

The PISA findings show a high degree of consistency within each country in the association between positive learning approaches and strong performance. Here, students' attitudes – their self-confidence and level of motivation – play a particularly important role alongside effective learning behaviour: the adoption of strong learning strategies. Strong attitudes are shown to be important for performance *both* in making it more likely that students will adopt fruitful strategies *and* in their own right independently of whether these strategies are actually adopted.

Students' approaches to learning impact on performance over and above the effect of family background. This is most obvious for motivational variables such as interest in reading and is also evident for students' beliefs in their own efficacy in some countries. Additionally, the data show that a large amount of the variability in performance associated with student background is also associated with the fact that students from more advantaged backgrounds tend to have stronger characteristics as learners. It is important thus to note that to reduce social disparities in performance it will be necessary to reduce the differences in student approaches to learning that appear to be behind much of these performance differences.

It is important however to bear in mind that only a fraction of the differences in student performance (about a fifth) are related to the variations in approaches to learning measured in PISA. The abilities being assessed depend also on a range of other factors including prior knowledge, capacity of the working memory and reasoning ability. All of these factors facilitate the process of comprehension when reading, as they free resources for deeper-level processing, meaning that new knowledge can be more easily integrated into the existing framework and hence more easily understood.

b) Student learning approaches as an outcome

Since it is desirable that students have strong approaches to learning when they leave school, regardless of whether it has already helped them to higher scholastic performance, the profile of students as learners is of interest in its own right. This report looked at such profiles in terms of the average strength of certain student characteristics in each country, the degree to which students clustered into groups with strengths or weaknesses across characteristics and the learning attributes of different sub-groups of the population.

Comparison of the mean values of the cross-nationally comparable scales of learner characteristics indicates that:

- Country differences in this respect are relatively small. To some extent, all countries face a similar situation.

- Differences across schools are also small when compared with differences within schools: relatively few schools succeed in promoting particularly strong approaches to learning among their students. Attention thus needs to be focused on teaching practices within schools and on system-wide change that improves these classroom practices.

- The cluster analysis presented in Chapter 3 identified a group of students with particularly strong motivation, self-confidence and learning strategies in combination and another particularly weak on these attributes. Clearly, the latter need targeted support – not just to help them succeed at school but also to equip them with learning attitudes and habits that will be important in their later lives. The fact that this clustering effect is of similar strength in all of the countries surveyed shows that no country can ignore the existence of students with multiple weaknesses.

c) Relationships between different learner characteristics

Effective, self-regulating learners cannot be created by fostering cognitive strategies alone. Learners also need to be reassured of being able to meet the challenges they will inevitably face and need to have the necessary motivation to deploy these strategies.

In all countries, students who tend to control their own learning processes and adapt them to the task at hand are characterised by a high level of confidence in their own abilities. Correlations with instrumental motivation and subject interest further indicate that students are more likely to use control strategies if they are motivated to learn by concrete incentives (*e.g.,* occupational aspirations) or specific interests. Overall, about two thirds of the differences in the degree to which students use these strategies can be explained by differences in motivation and self-related beliefs. Thus the attitudes and learning in behaviours of students are closely intertwined and a joined-up approach is needed to improve these characteristics as a whole. Again, the similarity of these relationships across countries indicates that these are general issues that all educational systems need to consider.

Implications for educational policy and practice

One of the main implications of the results presented in this report is that it is worthwhile for educational systems to promote students' ability to be effective and thus self-regulated learners. Students' approaches to learning, namely their use of learning strategies, their confidence and their motivation, are central aspects of schooling. They are not only associated with success in school but can also be viewed as an educational outcome as such. Students' motivation as well as their repertoire of strategies may change over life, but the prerequisites acquired in school function as a solid base for further development. Although there are no longitudinal studies that link students' capacity to regulate their own learning as measured in PISA with success in future life, evidence from the literature suggests that it indeed makes a difference. For example, university performance and grade levels have been shown to be dependent on students' use of strategies and interest and self-efficacy beliefs have been shown to exert a strong influence on strategy selection as well as on course selection and career profiles (see Artelt, 2000; Bandura, 1994; Baumert and Köller, 1998; Marsh and Craven, 1997; Schiefele, 1996).

This report's findings can give particular indications to educators about what aspects of approaches to learning are important in different respects. In particular:

• Of the learning strategies, *controlling* one's learning has the closest relationship with performance and is used most by stronger compared to weaker learners and also by female more than male students. *Elaboration* strategies are also related to performance, but tend (in countries where there are differences) to be used more by male students. This male tendency to process information and female tendency to think about what is being learned and relate it more to their goals shows that different learners have different strengths. Weaker readers and students from disadvantaged background are more on a level with their peers when it comes to *memorising* material. This can be seen partly as a feature of learning that can help such students' progress, but memorisation alone has limited potential to produce desired learning outcomes and it is thus important to foster comprehension-oriented strategies among all students. One important reason, arising from the PISA results, for aiming to create a more diverse range of learning strategies among students who are weakest in this regard is that students who control their learning to at least a modest extent tend to perform substantially better than those who do so little or not at all.

• Of the motivational characteristics, *interest in reading* has a particularly strong link with performance, which is largely independent of the fact that good readers are more likely to adopt certain strategies. Such an intrinsic motivation to learn, where it can be fostered, can help students considerably and again weaker readers and students from disadvantaged backgrounds are particularly likely to lack this characteristic. However, unlike use of control strategies, interest in reading is in many countries not associated strongly with performance when comparing students with little interest and with modest interest: it is only where interest is strong that it seems to make a big difference. On the other hand, reading interest is not the only significant feature of motivation and an external factor, *instrumental motivation* is particularly important in relation to the adoption of effective learning strategies. In most countries students with less advantaged backgrounds are no less likely to have such motivation at age 15. Thus even where it proves hard to create a strong love of learning for its own sake among students who have not had this message reinforced in their home and social environment, the evidence shows that students driven by factors such as job prospects are more likely to set and monitor learning goals and therefore give themselves a better chance of performing well. Here again there is a gender difference, with females more likely to be interested in reading but males being just as likely to have strong motivation from outside considerations. Schools and teachers thus need to look carefully at where there is greatest scope to foster stronger motivation and which type of motivation has the best chance of making a real difference to the learning perspectives and performance of each individual student.

• All aspects of students' self-related beliefs looked at in PISA are closely related to performance and in particular students who think that they can succeed in challenging or difficult learning tasks (*self-efficacy*) are more likely to adopt strong strategies and to perform at high levels of reading literacy. Interestingly, this characteristic is more prevalent in male than in female students; the latter derive greater confidence from their reading abilities (*self-concept in reading*). Here again, schools need to think carefully about the priority they give to building on students' strengths and to addressing areas of weakness.

• Student preferences for *competitive* or *co-operative* learning are not highly correlated with their performance, but each may play a role in different situations and in motivating different students. It appears that in some countries weaker students are particularly motivated by group, non-competitive learning situations and this is a preference to build on where it can be used to foster learning engagement.

Approaches to learning and implications for teaching

Students' ways of addressing learning tasks can be fostered, changed and modelled. This has important implications for attempts to reduce the performance gap between students from different family backgrounds.

Effective learning is a demanding activity. Students need to be able to figure out what they need to learn and how that goal can be reached. The literature on ways of instructing students in learning strategies has shown that the development of learning expertise is dependent not only on the existence of a repertoire of cognitive and metacognitive information-processing abilities but also on the readiness of individuals to define their own goals, to be proactive, to interpret success and failure appropriately, to translate wishes into intentions and plans and to shield learning from competing intentions (Weinert, 1994). Thus, students need to *learn how to learn*. From the perspective of teaching this implies that effective ways of learning, including goal setting, strategy selection and the control and evaluation of the learning process can and should be fostered by the educational setting and by teachers.

Students rarely learn how to learn on their own. Moreover, short-term interventions often fail to have positive effects. A repertoire of strategies combined with other attributes that foster learning develops gradually through teachers who model learning behaviour, through intricate activities aiming to build a scaffolding of learning for the student (Palincsar and Brown, 1984) and through analysis of reasons for academic success and failure. During the process of becoming effective and self-regulated learners, students need assistance and feedback, not only on the results of their learning, but also on the learning process itself. In particular, the one-fifth of students with generally weak approaches to learning in each of the 26 countries that participated in the study need professional assistance to become effective and self-regulated learners.

This report cannot tell education systems precisely how to address the needs of such learners. What it does tell is that they have to gear the way they deal with students to address aspects of attitudes and learning behaviours and to make these goals just as central to their mission as cognitive instruction. This may have implications for teacher training, as well as continuous professional development. Education systems also need to think about how they identify students with weaker characteristics as learners: PISA has shown that it is possible to distinguish them in a way that shows clear relationships with performance. The development of local tools for such assessment is a potential area for future research and development.

REFERENCES

Artelt, C. (2000). *Strategisches Lernen*. Münster: Waxmann.

Bandura, A. (1994). *Self-efficacy: The exercise of control*. New York: Freeman.

Baumert, J., Fend, H., O'Neil, H. and **Peschar J.** (1998). *Prepared for life-long learning*. Paris: OECD

Baumert, J. and **Köller, O.** (1998). Interest research in secondary level I: An Overview. In L. Hoffmann, A. Krapp, K.A. Renninger and J. Baumert, (Ed.), *Interest and learning*. Kiel: IPN.

Bempechat, J., Jimenez, NV. and **Boulay, B.A.** (2002), Cultural-cognitive issues in academic achievement: New directions for cross-national research. In A.C. Porter and A. Gamoran (Eds.), *Methodological advances in cross-national surveys of educational achievement* (117-149). Washington, D.C.: National Academic Press.

Boekaerts, M. (1997). Self-regulated learning: A new concept embraced by researchers, policy makers, educators, teachers and students. *Learning and Instruction*, 7(2), 161-186.

Boekaerts, M. (1999). Self-regulated learning: Where we are today. *International Journal of Educational Research*, 31, 445-475.

Bollen, K.A. (1989). *Structural equations with latent variables*. New York: John Wiley and Sons.

Brown, A. L., Bransford, J. D., Ferrara, R. A. and **Campione, J. C.** (1983). Learning, remembering and understanding. In J. H. Flavell and E. M. Markman (Hrsg.), *Handbook of child psychology. Cognitive development* (S. 77-166). New York: Wiley.

Corno, L. (1989). Self-regulated learning: A volitional analysis. In B.J. Zimmerman & D.H. Schunk (Eds.), Self regulated learning and academic achievement. Theory, research and practice (pp. 111-141). New York: Springer.

Czikszentmihalyi, M. (1985). *Das flow-Erlebnis. Jenseits von Angst und Langeweile: Im Tun aufgehen*. Stuttgart: Klett-Cotta.

Deci, E. L. and **Ryan, R. M.** (1985). *Intrinsic motivation and self-determination in human behavior*. New York: Plenum Press.

Dochy, F. J. R. C. (1996). Assessment of domain-specific and domain-transcending prior knowledge: Entry assessment and the use of profile analysis. In M. Birenbaum and F. J. R. C. Dochy (Hrsg.), *Alternatives in assessment of achievements, learning processes and prior knowledge* (S. 227-264). Boston: Kluwer Academic Publishers.

Eccles, J. S. (1994). Understanding women's educational and occupational choice: Applying the Eccles et al. model of achievement-related choices. *Psychology of Women Quarterly*, 18, 585-609.

Eccles, J. S. and **Wigfield, A.** (1995). In the mind of the achiever: The structure of adolescents' academic achievement related beliefs and self-perceptions. *Personality and Social Psychology Bulletin*, 21, 215-225.

Elley, W. B. E. (Ed.). (1994). *The IEA Study of Reading Literacy: Achievement and instruction in thirty-two school systems*. Oxford, UK: Pergamon.

Firebaugh, G. (1978). A rule for inferring individual-level relationships from aggregated data. *American Sociological Review*, 43, 557-572.

Flavell, J.H. and **Wellman, H.M.** (1977) Metamemory. In R.V. Kail, Jr. & W. Hagen (Eds), *Perspectives on development of memory and cognition* (pp. 3-31). Hillsdale, N.J.: Erlbaum.

Ganzeboom, H. B. G., de Graaf, P. M., Treiman, D. J., and **de Leeuw, J.** (1992). A standard international socio-economic index of occupational status. *Social Science Research*, 21, 1-56.

Guthrie, J. T. and **Wigfield, A**. (2000). Engagement and Motivation in Reading. In M. L. Kamil, P. Mosenthal, P. D. Pearson and R. B. (Eds.), *Handbook of Reading Research* (Vol. 3, pp. 403-422). Mahwah, NJ: Erlbaum.

Hansford, B.C. and **Hattie, J.A**. (1982). The relationship between self and achievement/performance measures. *Review of Educational Research*, 52, 123-142.

Hatano, G. (1998). Comprehension activity in individuals and groups. In M. Sabourin, F. Craik and M. Robert, (Ed.), *Advances in Psychological Science*. Volume 2: Biological and cognitive aspects, 399-418. Hove: Psychology Press/Erlbaum.

Heine, S.J., Lehman, D.R., Markus, H.R. and **Kitayama, S.** (1999). Is there a universal need for positive self-regard? *Psychological Review*, Vol. 106 (4), 766-794.

Holland, J.L. (1985) *Making Vocational Choices: A Theory of Vocational Personalities and Work Environments*. Englewood-Cliffs: Prentice Hall.

Hurrelmann, B. (1994). *Leseförderung*. Praxis Deutsch, 127, 17-26.

International Labor Office (1990). *International Standard Classification of Occupations*. ISCO-88. Geneva: International Labor Office.

Jöreskog, K.G. and **Sörbom, D.** (1988) *LISREL 7. A Guide to the program and applications*. Chicago: SPSS, Inc.

Lehtinen, E. (1992). Lern- und Bewältigungsstrategien im Unterricht. In H. Mandl and F.H. Friedrich (Eds.) *Lern und Denkstrategien: Analyse und Intervention* (p. 125-149) Göttingen: Hogrefe.

Marsh, H.W. (1986). Verbal and math self-concepts: An internal/external frame of reference model. *American Educational Research Journal*, 23, 129-149.

Marsh, H.W. (1993). The multidimensional structure of academic self-concept: Invariance over gender and age. *American Educational Research Journal*, 30 (4), 841-860.

Marsh, H.W. and **Craven** (1997). Academic self-concept: Beyond the dustbowl, In G.D. Phye (Ed.), *Handbook of classroom assessment* (pp. 137-198). San Diego, CA: Academic Press.

Marsh, H.W. and **Hau, K.T.** (2002). Paradoxical relations between academic self-concepts and achievement: *Generalisability of the Internal-External frame of reference in 26 countries*. (in preparation).

Marsh, H.W., Shavelson, R. J. and **Byrne, B. M.** (1992). A multidimensional, hierarchical self-concept. In R. P. Lipka and T. M. Brinthaupt (Eds.), *Studying the self: Perspectives across the life-span*.

O'Neil, H. F. and **Herl, H. E.** (1998). *Reliability and validity of a trait measure of self-regulation*. UCLA/CRESST AERA.

Organisation for Economic Co-operation and Development (1997). *Prepared for Life? How to measure Cross-Curricular competencies* (Bilingual). Paris: OECD

Organisation for Economic Co-operation and Development (1999). *Measuring student knowledge and skills: A new framework for assessment*. Paris: OECD.

Organisation for Economic Co-operation and Development (2001). *Knowledge and Skills for Life. First Results from PISA 2000*. Paris: OECD.

Organisation for Economic Co-operation and Development (2002a). *PISA 2000 Technical Report*. Paris: OECD

Organisation for Economic Co-operation and Development (2002b). *Reading for Change: Performance and engagement across countries*. Paris: OECD.

Organisation for Economic Co-operation and Development (2002c). *Education Policy Analysis*. Paris: OECD.

Palincsar, A.S. and **Brown, A. L.** (1984). Reciprocal teaching of comprehension-fostering and comprehension-monitoring activities. *Cognition and Instruction*, 1(2), 117 – 175.

Paris, S.G and **Byrnes, J.** (1989). The constructivist approach to self-regulation and learning in the classroom. In B.J. Zimmerman and D.H. Schunk (Ed.), *Self-regulated learning and academic achievement. Theory, research and practice* (169-200). New York: Springer Verlag.

Peschar, J. Veenstra, R. and **Molenaar, I.W.** (1999). *Self-Regulated learning as a Cross-Curricular Competency. The Construction of Instruments in 22 Countries for the PISA Main Study 2000*. Washington, DC: American Institutes of Research (AIR).

Pressley, M, Borkowski, J.G. and **Schneider, W.** (1987). Cognitive strategy user coordinate metacognition and knowledge. In R. Vasta and G. Whitehurst (Eds.), *Annals of child development* (89-129). New York: Jai Press.

Pressley, M, Borkowski, J.G. and **Schneider, W.** (1989). Good information processing: What it is and how education can promote it. *International Journal of Educational Research*, 13, 857-867.

Robinson, W. S. (1950). Ecological correlations and the behaviour of individuals. *American Sociological Review*, 28, 399-411.

Rosenshine, B. and **Meister, C.** (1994). Reciprocal teaching. A review of the research. *Review of Educational Research*, 64, 479-531.

Rychen, D.S. and **L. H. Salganik** (2002) (Eds) *Defining and Selecting Key Competencies* (Hogrefe and Huber Publishers: Seattle.

Schiefele, U. (1996) *Motivation und Lernen mit Texten.* Göttingen: Hogrefe.

Schiefele, U., Krapp, A. and **Winteler, A**. (1992). Interest as predictor of academic achievement: A meta-analysis of research. In K. A. Renninger, S. Hidi and A. K. (Eds.) , *The role of interest in learning and development* (pp. 183-212). Hillsdale, NJ: Erlbaum.

Schneider, W. (1989). *Zur Entwicklung des Metagedächtnisses bei Kindern.* Bern : Huber.

Schneider, W. (1996). Zum Zusammenhang zwischen Metakognition und Motivation bei Lern- und Gedächtnisvorgängen. In C. Spiel, U. Kastner-Koller and P. Deimann (Hrsg.), *Motivation und Lernen aus der Perspektive lebenslanger Entwicklung* (S. 121-133). Münster: Waxmann.

Schneider, W. and **Pressley, M.** (1997). *Memory development between two and twenty.* (2nd Edition). Mahwah: Erlbaum.

Simons, P. R. J. (1992). Lernen selbständig zu lernen - ein Rahmenmodell. In H. Mandl and H. F. Friedrich (Hrsg.), *Lern- und Denkstrategien. Analyse und Intervention* (S. 251-264). Göttingen: Hogrefe.

van de Vijver, F. and **Leung, K.** (1997) Methods and data analysis of comparative research. In J. W. Berry, Y., H. Poortinga and J. Pandey (Eds.). *Handbook of cross-cultural psychology.* Vol 1 Theory and method. (257-300). Needham Heights, MA: Allyn and Bacon.

van de Vijver, F. and **Tanzer, N.K.** (1998). Bias and equivalence in cross-cultural assessment : An overview. *European Review of Applied Psychology*, 47, 263-279.

Veenman, M. V. J. and **van Hout-Wolters, B. H. A. M.** (2002). Het meten van metacognitieve vaardigheden. In F. Daems, R. Rymenans, & G. Rogiest, (Eds.), *Onderwijsonderzoek in Nederland en Vlaanderen. Prooceedings van de 29e Onderwijs Research Dagen 2002 te Antwerpen* (pp. 102-103). Antwerpen: Universiteit Antwerpen.

Warm, T.A. (1985). *Weighted maximum likelihood estimation of ability in Item Response Theory with tests of finite length* (Technical Report CGI-TR-85-08). Oklahoma City: U.S. Coast Guard Institute.

Weinert, F. E. (1994). Lernen lernen und das eigene lernen verstehen. In K. Reusser and M. Reusser-Weyeneth (Hrsg.), Verstehen. *Psychologischer Prozeß und didaktische Aufgabe* (S. 183-205). Bern: Huber.

Wigfield, A., Eccles, J. S. and **Rodriguez, D.** (1998). The development of children's motivation in school contexts. In P. D. Pearson. and A. Iran-Nejad (Eds.), *Review of research in education* (Vol. 23, 73-118). Washington DC: American Educational Research Association.

Willoughby, T. and **Wood, E.** (1994). Elaborative interrogation examined at encoding and retrieval. *Learning and Instruction*, 4, 139-149.

Winne, P.H. (2001). Self-regulated learning viewed from models of information processing. In B.J. Zimmerman and D.H. Schunk (Eds.), *Self-regulated learning and academic achievement: theoretical perspectives* (pp 153 – 189) Mahwah, NJ: Erlbaum

Zimmerman, B. J. (1989). Models of self-regulated learning and academic achievement. In B. J. Zimmerman and D. H. Schunk (Ed.), *Self-regulated learning and academic achievement. Theory, research and practice* (S. 1-25), New York: Springer-Verlag.

Zimmerman, B.J. (1999). Commentary: toward a cyclically interactive view of self-regulated learning. *International Journal of Educational Research*, 31, 545-551.

Zimmerman, B. J. and **Martinez-Pons, M.** (1990). Student differences in self-regulated learning: Relating grade, sex and giftedness to self-efficacy and strategy use. *Journal of Educational Psychology*, 82(1), 51-59.

Zimmerman, B.J. and **Schunk, D.H.** (2001) (Eds.), *Self-regulated learning and academic achievement: Theoretical perspectives.* Mahwah: Erlbaum.

PISA QUESTIONNAIRE ITEMS MEASURING STUDENT CHARACTERISTICS AS LEARNERS

Learning strategies

Elaboration strategies

	almost never	some-times	often	almost always
When I study, I try to relate new material to things I have learned in other subjects..........................	☐	☐	☐	☐
When I study, I figure out how the information might be useful in the real world...............................	☐	☐	☐	☐
When I study, I try to understand the material better by relating it to things I already know.................	☐	☐	☐	☐
When I study, I figure out how the material fits in with what I have learned...................................	☐	☐	☐	☐

Memorisation strategies

	almost never	some-times	often	almost always
When I study, I try to memorise everything that might be covered...	☐	☐	☐	☐
When I study, I memorise as much as possible................	☐	☐	☐	☐
When I study, I memorise all new material so that I can recite it..	☐	☐	☐	☐
When I study, I practice by saying the material to myself over and over...	☐	☐	☐	☐

Control strategies

	almost never	some-times	often	almost always
When I study, I start by figuring out what exactly I need to learn...	☐	☐	☐	☐
When I study, I force myself to check to see if I remember what I have learned.............................	☐	☐	☐	☐
When I study, I try to figure out, as I read, which concepts I still haven't really understood......................	☐	☐	☐	☐
When I study, I make sure that I remember the most important things..	☐	☐	☐	☐
When I study, and I don't understand something, I look for additional information to clarify the point.........	☐	☐	☐	☐

Motivation

Instrumental motivation

	almost never	some- times	often	almost always
I study to increase my job opportunities........................	☐	☐	☐	☐
I study to ensure that my future will be financially secure...	☐	☐	☐	☐
I study to get a good job..	☐	☐	☐	☐

Interest in reading

	disagree	disagree somewhat	agree somewhat	agree
Because reading is fun, I wouldn't want to give it up.........	☐	☐	☐	☐
I read in my spare time..	☐	☐	☐	☐
When I read, I sometimes get totally absorbed................	☐	☐	☐	☐

Interest in mathematics

	disagree	disagree somewhat	agree somewhat	agree
When I do mathematics, I sometimes get totally absorbed..	☐	☐	☐	☐
Mathematics is important to me personally....................	☐	☐	☐	☐
Because doing mathematics is fun, I wouldn't want to give it up.	☐	☐	☐	☐

Effort and persistence in learning

	almost never	some- times	often	almost always
When studying. I work as hard as possible.....................	☐	☐	☐	☐
When studying, I keep working even if the material is difficult..	☐	☐	☐	☐
When studying, I try to do my best to acquire the knowledge and skills taught......................................	☐	☐	☐	☐
When studying, I put forth my best effort.....................	☐	☐	☐	☐

Self-related beliefs

Self-efficacy

	almost never	some-times	often	almost always
I'm certain I can understand the most difficult material presented in readings..................................	☐	☐	☐	☐
I'm confident I can understand the most complex material presented by the teacher...............................	☐	☐	☐	☐
I'm confident I can do an excellent job on assignments and tests...	☐	☐	☐	☐
I'm certain I can master the skills being taught................	☐	☐	☐	☐

Self-concept of verbal competencies

	disagree	disagree somewhat	agree somewhat	agree
I'm hopeless in <test language> classes (*Reversed*).............	☐	☐	☐	☐
When I do mathematics, I sometimes get totally absorbed..	☐	☐	☐	☐
Mathematics is important to me personally....................	☐	☐	☐	☐
Because doing mathematics is fun. I wouldn't want to give it up..	☐	☐	☐	☐

Self-concept of mathematical competencies

	disagree	disagree somewhat	agree somewhat	agree
I get good marks in mathematics................................	☐	☐	☐	☐
Mathematics is one of my best subjects.........................	☐	☐	☐	☐
I have always done well in mathematics........................	☐	☐	☐	☐

Academic self-concept

	disagree	disagree somewhat	agree somewhat	agree
I learn things quickly in most school subjects..................	☐	☐	☐	☐
I do well in tests in most school subjects.......................	☐	☐	☐	☐
I'm good at most school subjects................................	☐	☐	☐	☐

Self-report of social competencies

Preference for co-operative learning

	disagree	disagree somewhat	agree somewhat	agree
I like to work with other students...............................	☐	☐	☐	☐
I learn the most when I work with other students............	☐	☐	☐	☐
I do my best work when I work with other students.........	☐	☐	☐	☐
I like to help other people do well in a group..................	☐	☐	☐	☐
It is helpful to put together everyone's ideas when working on a project......................................	☐	☐	☐	☐

Preference for competitive learning

	disagree	disagree somewhat	agree somewhat	agree
I like to try to be better than other students...................	☐	☐	☐	☐
Trying to be better than others makes me work well........	☐	☐	☐	☐
I would like to be the best at something........................	☐	☐	☐	☐
I learn faster if I'm trying to do better than the others..	☐	☐	☐	☐

Annex

BACKGROUND TO SCALES MEASURING LEARNER CHARACTERISTICS

Psychometric quality of learner characteristics scales

The central precondition for the analysis of the patterns of interaction between the various learner characteristics examined in PISA, as well as for the subgroup comparisons, is that the instruments function properly and are suitable for the purposes of an international comparison. The reliability and validity of the scales must thus be tested at various levels. The first step in this procedure is to test the structural equivalence and psychometric characteristics of the scales used to measure self-regulated learning. The second step is to test the extent to which level-based comparisons of the scales – i.e., comparisons of means – are admissible. The quality and, to some extent, cross-cultural comparability of the instruments designed to measure the prerequisites of self-regulated learning were tested in the PISA field trial (Peschar, Veenstra and Molenaar, 1999). The reliability of the scales proves to be satisfactory. The reliability coefficients are, on average, all above 0.7; for three scales they are even above 0.8. Within the countries, too, the reliabilities are high enough to meet common quality standards; the reliability coefficients were somewhat low in only four of the 338 cases tested (see Table C2.1)[1]. In a further step to test the structural equivalence of the self-regulated learning scales across the 26 countries, confirmatory factor analysis was used to investigate whether the constructs under examination (e.g., self-concept, interest, learning strategies) cover the same meaning across countries. The results of these analyses are presented

Figure B2.1
Assumed model for the scales on self-related cognitions

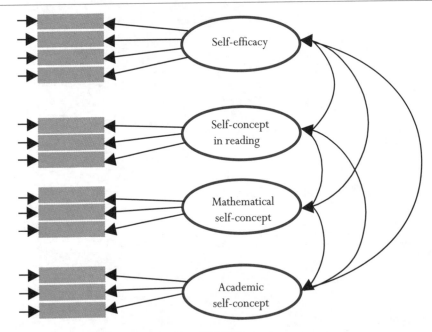

Table B2.1
Goodness of Fit statistics for the multiple group comparison for the scales on self-related cognitions

General invariance constraints[1]	chi^2	chi^2/df	df	RMSEA*	CFI**	TLI***
None (totally free)	24 413	15.91	1 534	0.011	0.958	0.934
Invariance of factor loadings	27 565	15.67	1 759	0.011	0.952	0.936
Invariance of factor loadings and factor correlations	30 841	16.15	1 909	0.011	0.946	0.933
Invariance of factor loadings, factor correlations and factor variances	33 174	16.51	2 009	0.011	0.942	0.932

1. Parameters are constrained to be the same across all 26 groups.
* RMSEA= Root Mean Square Error of Approximation.
** CFI= Comparative Fit Index.
*** TLI=Tucker-Lewis Index.

Figure B2.2
Assumed model for the scales on motivation/volition and learning preferences

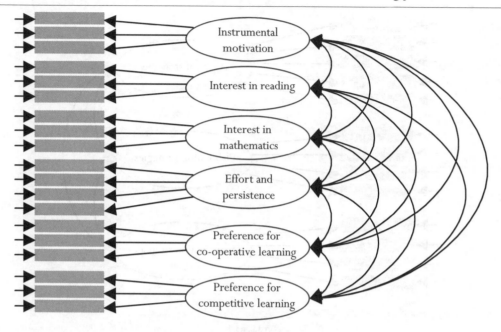

Table B2.2
Goodness of Fit statistics for the multiple group comparison for the scales on motivation/volition and learning preferences

General invariance constraints[1]	chi^2	chi^2/df	df	RMSEA[*]	CFI[**]	TLI[***]
None (totally free)	29 137	8.18	3 562	0.008	0.963	0.949
Invariance of factor loadings	33 587	8.64	3 887	0.008	0.957	0.946
Invariance of factor loadings and factor correlations	39 312	9.22	1 172	0.008	0.950	0.942
Invariance of factor loadings, factor correlations and factor variances	43 713	9.90	1 022	0.009	0.944	0.937

1. Parameters are constrained to be the same across all 26 groups.
[*] RMSEA= Root Mean Square Error of Approximation.
[**] CFI= Comparative Fit Index.
[***] TLI= Tucker-Lewis Index.

in detail in Tables B2.1 to B 2.3 and Figures B2.1 to B2.3. These tests of the structural equivalence of the scales confirm that the structure of the scales is generally invariant across countries. Thus, irrespective of the cultural background of students in different participating countries, the items used to measure self-regulated learning in PISA tap comparable concepts (see also OECD 2002*a*).

The assumption of structural equivalence was tested by means of a multi-group confirmatory factor analysis design that allows factorial invariance to be tested across groups (Bollen, 1989; Jöreskog and Sörbom, 1988). The minimal criterion for structural equivalence is that the factor loading relating each indicator to its hypothesised factor is the same across all countries participating in the optional survey on self-regulated learning. Before testing the assumption of equal factor loadings, the scales for self-regulated learning were grouped into three theoretically based categories: (*i*) self-related cognitions, (*ii*) motivation/volition and learning preferences and (*iii*) learning strategies. Figures B2.1 to B2.3. demonstrate the models for each of the three groups. Tables B2.1 to B2.3 present the results of the multi-

Figure B2.3
Assumed model for the scales on learning strategies

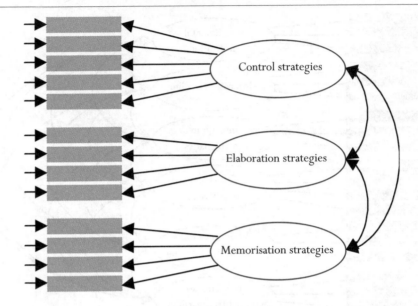

Table B2.3
Goodness of Fit statistics for the multiple group comparison for the scales on learning strategies

General invariance constraints[1]	chi²	chi²/df	df	RMSEA*	CFI**	TLI***
None (totally free)	36 439	22.60	1 612	0.013	0.919	0.881
Invariance of factor loadings	41 676	22.38	1 862	0.013	0.907	0.882
Invariance of factor loadings and factor correlations	45 808	23.65	1 937	0.014	0.898	0.875
Invariance of factor loadings, factor correlations and factor variances	53 105	26.39	2 012	0.015	0.881	0.860

1. Parameters are constrained to be the same across all 26 groups.
* RMSEA= Root Mean Square Error of Approximation.
** CFI= Comparative Fit Index.
*** TLI= Tucker-Lewis Index.

group models with varying parameter constraints. The first model in each table tests the model illustrated in the figures, without any assumption being made about parameter invariance across groups. In other words, the first model tests whether the indicators (items) in each of the scales group in accordance with the theoretical expectations. The second model presented in each of the three tables tests the assumption that the factor loadings are invariant across groups, *i.e.*, that the relative weight and height of each factor indicator is the same across groups. For our purposes, the assumption of factor loading invariance is the crucial point. The models presented in Tables B2.1 to B2.3 increase the number of invariance constraints across groups. In addition to equal factor loadings, the subsequent two models test the assumption that factor correlations (third model) and – finally – factor variances (fourth model) are equal across countries.

The decision as to which solution based on a particular model adequately fits the data was based on whether the iterative procedure converges to proper solutions, and on a comparison of the fit statistics for the competing models (omnibus test) presented in Tables B2.1 to B2.3 (Marsh, 1993). According to two of four the indicators presented (RMSEA and TLI), the model assuming equal factor loadings is the best fit for the scales on self-related cognitions (Table B2.1) The test for the motivation/volition and learning preference model indicates that the assumption of equal factor loading is not the best solution, and that the constraint-free model has a better fit. Nevertheless, the decrease in fit-indices is rather small, and RMSEA is the same in both groups. The model for the scales on learning strategies indicates that the assumption of invariant factor structure is well founded. Three of the four fit-indices (chi^2/df, RMSEA, TLI) support this model.

Taken together, the omnibus test of factorial invariance across groups indicates that the assumption of equal factor loading holds in two of the three domains, but that for the model on motivation/volition and learning preferences, the situation is not so straightforward.

Finally, Table B2.4 presents the reliability coefficients for each of the scales on learner characteristics in the 26 countries. In line with the results presented above, this pattern of results indicates that there are good reasons to assume structural equivalence of the scales (in the sense of factorial invariance) across the 26 countries.

Aggregate variables often measure a different construct than their namesake at the individual level. Often, the aggregate-level variable taps more constructs than the individual-level variable[2]. Such a shift in constructs can indeed be shown for some of the PISA self-regulated learning scales – cultural influences are very probable here.

The question of whether concepts of self-regulated learning imply something different on the country level than on the individual level was tested by means of multilevel modelling. To this end, cross-level effects were calculated by hierarchical linear modelling (HLM) using students' scores on the combined reading literacy test as Y in the formula $Y = a + \beta_1 x_1 + \beta_2 \bar{X}_1 + e$. According to Firebaugh (1978), cross-level bias is absent when, and only when, $\beta_2 = 0$ which means that the regression coefficients at the individual and the country level do not differ significantly ($\beta_{\bar{YX}} - \beta_{yx}$ n.s.). If cross-level bias is absent, scores on the self-regulated learning scales can be interpreted in the same way at the country level as at the individual level (see Tables B2.4 and A3.2). It cannot be assumed, however, that the lack of a significant cross-level

Table B2.4
Learner characteristics scales with no significant cross-level bias:
individual-level and country-level effects[1] on the combined reading literacy scale

	Significant cross-level bias		
	Individual-level effect	Country-level effect	Cross-level bias
Elaboration strategies	18.76	-196.39	-215.15 **
Control strategies	32.78	-50.75	-83.53 **
Instrumental motivation	9.17	-78.89	-88.06 **
Interest in reading	28.91	-97.73	-126.64 **
Interest in mathematics	6.18	-111.58	-117.76 **
Academic self-concept	38.9	-11.43	-50.33 *
Effort and persistence	19.95	-124.98	-144.93 *
Preference for competitive learning	11.73	-139.96	-151.69 **

1. Unstandardised regression coefficient.
* $p<0.05$.
** $p<0.01$.

Table B2.5
Learner characteristics scales with no significant cross-level bias:
individual-level and country-level effects[1] on the combined reading literacy scale

	Non-significant cross-level bias		
	Individual-level effect	Country-level effect	Cross-level bias
Memorisation strategies	2.01	-13.67	-15.68
Self-efficacy	33.67	-117.86	-151.53
Self-concept in reading	31.94	-39.01	-70.95
Mathematical self-concept	14.83	-28.58	-43.41
Preference for co-operative learning	-5.10	-6.67	-1.57

1. Unstandardised regression coefficient.

effect would prove the concepts to be identical. It may be that other effects would emerge to be significant if a different criterion were chosen. The criterion "relationship to reading literacy" was selected here because of its central importance in PISA.

No significant cross-level bias emerged for any of the other self-regulated learning scales in the multi-level analysis (Table B2.5). None of the effects tested are significant.

The fact that no cross-level bias was found for these scales with respect to reading literacy does not exclude the possibility that a shift in constructs might be observed if another criterion (*e.g.*, nations' cumulative expenditure per student) were considered. Nevertheless, for the evaluation of self-regulated learning the relationships with achievement are considered to be a more relevant criterion.

Notes

1. The internal consistency of the memorisation strategies scale in Latvia and the Russian Federation and of the instrumental motivation and self-concept in reading scales in Mexico is between 0.5 and 0.6.

DATA TABLES

Table C2.1
Cronbach's Alpha (reliability) for the scales showing learner characteristics

		Memorisation strategies	Elaboration strategies	Control strategies	Instrumental motivation	Interest in reading	Interest in mathematics	Self-efficacy	Self-concept in reading	Mathematical self-concept	Academic self-concept	Effort and persistence	Preference for co-opertivelearning	Preference for competitive learning
OECD COUNTRIES	Australia	0.74	0.79	0.81	0.83	0.83	0.72	0.79	0.76	0.86	0.74	0.81	0.75	0.80
	Austria	0.71	0.74	0.68	0.81	0.84	0.72	0.74	0.81	0.88	0.76	0.76	0.80	0.76
	Belgium (Fl.)	0.76	0.77	0.69	0.84	0.88	0.78	0.72	0.72	0.85	0.70	0.78	0.69	0.78
	Czech Republic	0.74	0.79	0.76	0.81	0.86	0.68	0.75	0.75	0.84	0.76	0.75	0.74	0.74
	Denmark	0.63	0.76	0.71	0.79	0.85	0.83	0.79	0.78	0.87	0.80	0.76	0.76	0.81
	Finland	0.71	0.80	0.77	0.82	0.88	0.81	0.83	0.80	0.93	0.84	0.78	0.76	0.82
	Germany	0.73	0.75	0.73	0.83	0.85	0.76	0.75	0.82	0.90	0.78	0.77	0.77	0.75
	Hungary	0.72	0.78	0.73	0.85	0.87	0.74	0.79	0.66	0.87	0.73	0.76	0.79	0.71
	Iceland	0.70	0.77	0.72	0.82	0.78	0.66	0.84	0.77	0.90	0.81	0.77	0.82	0.79
	Ireland	0.75	0.78	0.78	0.85	0.84	0.71	0.80	0.79	0.87	0.77	0.82	0.79	0.83
	Italy	0.67	0.80	0.75	0.84	0.82	0.72	0.76	0.82	0.87	0.74	0.78	0.79	0.78
	Korea	0.70	0.76	0.72	0.72	0.83	0.83	0.76	0.67	0.90	0.77	0.78	0.65	0.75
	Luxembourg	0.77	0.76	0.77	0.82	0.81	0.72	0.76	0.73	0.87	0.74	0.78	0.76	0.74
	Mexico	0.75	0.77	0.74	0.69	0.61	0.50	0.75	0.54	0.84	0.71	0.74	0.77	0.67
	New Zealand	0.74	0.77	0.80	0.85	0.83	0.75	0.78	0.81	0.89	0.79	0.80	0.77	0.83
	Norway	0.77	0.80	0.75	0.83	0.85	0.79	0.81	0.74	0.90	0.84	0.79	0.82	0.83
	Portugal	0.73	0.74	0.77	0.84	0.81	0.73	0.76	0.74	0.87	0.73	0.78	0.73	0.82
	Scotland	0.68	0.74	0.75	0.79	0.86	0.71	0.78	0.81	0.87	0.74	0.76	0.74	0.84
	Sweden	0.74	0.80	0.76	0.85	0.75	0.77	0.81	0.75	0.88	0.81	0.80	0.81	0.84
	Switzerland	0.70	0.75	0.74	0.78	0.84	0.77	0.71	0.76	0.88	0.74	0.79	0.73	0.77
	United States	0.77	0.81	0.83	0.83	0.82	0.74	0.83	0.76	0.86	0.79	0.83	0.82	0.81
	OECD average	*0.71*	*0.77*	*0.73*	*0.82*	*0.82*	*0.75*	*0.77*	*0.73*	*0.88*	*0.78*	*0.78*	*0.76*	*0.78*
NON-OECD COUNTRIES	Brazil	0.67	0.73	0.77	0.83	0.73	0.66	0.75	0.61	0.85	0.73	0.77	0.75	0.75
	Latvia	0.54	0.63	0.66	0.70	0.75	0.72	0.67	0.67	0.85	0.66	0.70	0.72	0.66
	Liechtenstein	0.72	0.80	0.78	0.83	0.84	0.73	0.73	0.73	0.84	0.77	0.81	0.77	0.70
	Russian Federation	0.56	0.77	0.72	0.76	0.78	0.75	0.76	0.67	0.87	0.72	0.76	0.75	0.71
	Netherlands[1]	0.65	0.76	0.70	0.82	0.84	0.76	0.72	0.74	0.89	0.76	0.77	0.69	0.80

1. Response rate is too low to ensure comparability.

Table C2.2
Performance on the combined reading literacy scale by national quarters of the index of control strategies

		Bottom quarter		Second quarter		Third quarter		Top quarter	
		Mean	S.E.	Mean	S.E.	Mean	S.E.	Mean	S.E.
OECD COUNTRIES	Australia	495	(4.4)	523	(4.9)	537	(4.4)	565	(5.3)
	Austria	488	(3.7)	505	(3.4)	520	(3.3)	532	(3.5)
	Belgium (Fl.)	517	(7.0)	542	(4.1)	544	(5.1)	544	(5.5)
	Czech Republic	465	(3.2)	497	(3.0)	518	(3.3)	531	(2.8)
	Denmark	484	(3.3)	499	(4.8)	506	(3.4)	516	(3.1)
	Finland	526	(3.8)	550	(2.9)	559	(4.0)	562	(3.6)
	Germany	460	(4.4)	498	(3.9)	508	(3.6)	521	(3.1)
	Hungary	457	(5.8)	483	(4.4)	496	(4.5)	497	(5.7)
	Iceland	490	(3.3)	509	(3.2)	515	(3.3)	527	(3.6)
	Ireland	498	(4.5)	524	(4.6)	536	(3.9)	554	(3.8)
	Italy	461	(5.1)	486	(3.8)	499	(3.4)	505	(3.1)
	Korea	498	(3.2)	523	(2.9)	535	(3.2)	549	(2.9)
	Luxembourg	425	(3.4)	450	(3.3)	464	(2.9)	478	(3.6)
	Mexico	394	(3.7)	415	(3.7)	435	(4.6)	449	(4.9)
	New Zealand	494	(4.4)	528	(3.6)	540	(3.6)	571	(4.8)
	Norway	494	(5.7)	505	(3.9)	522	(4.2)	520	(3.9)
	Portugal	421	(5.6)	470	(4.6)	486	(4.5)	517	(4.3)
	Scotland	493	(5.4)	521	(5.2)	531	(5.7)	555	(4.6)
	Sweden	489	(3.4)	513	(3.3)	525	(4.0)	538	(2.6)
	Switzerland	473	(4.7)	492	(4.8)	511	(5.3)	522	(6.2)
	United States	473	(7.1)	505	(8.5)	530	(5.5)	534	(8.1)
	OECD average	475	(1.1)	499	(1.1)	513	(1.0)	528	(1.1)
NON-OECD COUNTRIES	Brazil	369	(4.2)	396	(4.1)	415	(4.0)	426	(4.3)
	Latvia	432	(6.5)	462	(6.2)	470	(6.8)	484	(5.6)
	Liechtenstein	460	(11.5)	477	(10.4)	479	(10.0)	524	(9.7)
	Russian Federation	429	(5.3)	458	(4.9)	472	(4.3)	487	(4.5)
	Netherlands[1]	508	(5.7)	540	(4.2)	539	(3.7)	539	(5.5)

1. Response rate is too low to ensure comparability.

Table C2.3
Performance on the combined reading literacy scale by national quarters of the index of interest in reading

		Bottom quarter		Second quarter		Third quarter		Top quarter	
		Mean	S.E.	Mean	S.E.	Mean	S.E.	Mean	S.E.
OECD COUNTRIES	Australia	494	(3.9)	508	(5.3)	540	(4.3)	595	(4.6)
	Austria	481	(3.1)	486	(3.5)	514	(3.5)	556	(3.4)
	Belgium (Fl.)	515	(4.5)	518	(5.9)	531	(5.9)	571	(5.5)
	Czech Republic	472	(2.6)	484	(2.9)	512	(3.2)	549	(3.1)
	Denmark	472	(3.2)	485	(3.5)	502	(3.9)	550	(3.4)
	Finland	505	(2.6)	530	(5.3)	563	(2.9)	598	(3.1)
	Germany	469	(3.5)	471	(3.8)	497	(4.4)	550	(3.6)
	Hungary	453	(4.1)	466	(5.1)	492	(4.8)	524	(4.7)
	Iceland	473	(3.1)	494	(2.9)	514	(3.3)	561	(3.4)
	Ireland	496	(3.8)	498	(4.5)	536	(4.0)	580	(3.6)
	Italy	466	(3.9)	470	(4.9)	492	(3.6)	522	(3.1)
	Korea	492	(2.9)	519	(3.2)	535	(3.5)	552	(2.6)
	Luxembourg	446	(2.9)	439	(3.6)	452	(3.0)	491	(3.5)
	Mexico	423	(4.4)	420	(3.9)	419	(3.7)	437	(5.2)
	New Zealand	508	(3.7)	510	(3.6)	543	(4.6)	598	(4.4)
	Norway	473	(4.7)	487	(4.2)	519	(3.5)	571	(3.2)
	Portugal	441	(4.7)	454	(6.5)	472	(4.7)	513	(4.6)
	Scotland	490	(5.2)	501	(5.0)	528	(6.7)	581	(4.7)
	Sweden	479	(3.1)	503	(2.7)	529	(4.1)	570	(2.9)
	Switzerland	464	(4.1)	476	(4.5)	501	(5.2)	552	(5.4)
	United States	490	(8.1)	492	(7.1)	506	(7.6)	557	(6.7)
	OECD average	*475*	*(0.8)*	*484*	*(1.1)*	*509*	*(1.0)*	*549*	*(1.0)*
NON-OECD COUNTRIES	Brazil	396	(3.8)	403	(4.0)	397	(4.6)	419	(4.4)
	Latvia	429	(6.4)	443	(7.2)	463	(5.3)	513	(5.6)
	Liechtenstein	451	(10.0)	467	(10.0)	489	(10.1)	539	(10.1)
	Russian Federation	442	(4.7)	452	(3.8)	468	(5.0)	499	(5.0)
	Netherlands[1]	509	(4.7)	517	(4.6)	535	(5.4)	573	(4.6)

1. Response rate is too low to ensure comparability.

Table C2.4
Performance on the combined reading literacy scale by national quarters of the index of self-efficacy

	Bottom quarter		Second quarter		Third quarter		Top quarter	
	Mean	S.E.	Mean	S.E.	Mean	S.E.	Mean	S.E.
Australia	506	(4.5)	520	(5.2)	536	(4.1)	571	(4.7)
Austria	483	(4.0)	503	(4.0)	513	(3.1)	536	(3.7)
Belgium (Fl.)	514	(8.4)	535	(4.4)	543	(4.6)	552	(6.5)
Czech Republic	486	(2.7)	499	(3.5)	510	(3.2)	526	(3.8)
Denmark	465	(3.6)	490	(4.0)	500	(3.2)	544	(2.6)
Finland	525	(3.1)	535	(3.7)	549	(3.0)	583	(4.1)
Germany	470	(4.2)	492	(3.5)	506	(3.8)	527	(4.9)
Hungary	464	(5.5)	477	(4.5)	490	(6.1)	500	(5.1)
Iceland	471	(3.0)	504	(3.3)	522	(3.7)	556	(3.5)
Ireland	506	(4.3)	521	(4.6)	531	(4.0)	555	(4.3)
Italy	472	(4.9)	481	(3.4)	496	(3.3)	506	(4.4)
Korea	498	(3.4)	520	(3.3)	528	(2.8)	549	(3.0)
Luxembourg	434	(2.9)	449	(3.9)	461	(3.1)	475	(3.3)
Mexico	402	(3.3)	415	(4.1)	425	(4.3)	447	(5.4)
New Zealand	509	(4.8)	529	(3.9)	538	(4.1)	575	(5.3)
Norway	475	(4.2)	499	(3.8)	515	(5.7)	554	(3.6)
Portugal	442	(5.3)	459	(5.5)	473	(5.3)	505	(4.9)
Scotland	504	(5.6)	513	(5.8)	535	(4.4)	562	(5.6)
Sweden	480	(3.1)	505	(3.3)	528	(3.3)	560	(3.4)
Switzerland	471	(4.4)	495	(5.2)	499	(5.5)	520	(5.1)
United States	474	(7.4)	510	(7.1)	518	(6.9)	548	(8.3)
OECD average	*476*	*(0.9)*	*498*	*(1.1)*	*509*	*(0.9)*	*532*	*(1.1)*
Brazil	376	(3.8)	395	(3.8)	411	(4.3)	432	(4.7)
Latvia	434	(5.7)	457	(6.2)	467	(6.2)	494	(6.6)
Liechtenstein	446	(11.0)	475	(7.4)	514	(8.8)	507	(11.8)
Russian Federation	435	(4.9)	458	(4.9)	470	(3.5)	492	(5.0)
Netherlands[1]	517	(5.4)	526	(3.9)	543	(5.4)	545	(4.5)

(Left margin labels: OECD COUNTRIES; NON-OECD COUNTRIES)

1. Response rate is too low to ensure comparability.

Table C2.5a
Relationships between memorisation strategies and learner characteristics (standardised regression coefficients * and standard errors)

	Elaboration strategies		Control strategies		Instrumental motivation		Interest in reading		Interest in mathematics		Self-efficacy		Self-concept in reading		Mathematical self-concept		Academic self-concept		Effort and persistence		Preference for co-operative learning		Preference for competitive learning	
	Index	S.E.	Index	S.E.	Index	S.E.	Index	S.E.	Index	S.E.	Index	S.E.	Index	S.E.	Index	S.E.	Index	S.E.	Index	S.E.	Index	S.E.	Index	S.E.
OECD COUNTRIES																								
Australia	0.54	(0.02)	0.70	(0.01)	0.50	(0.01)	0.16	(0.02)	0.29	(0.01)	0.52	(0.02)	0.23	(0.02)	0.21	(0.02)	0.33	(0.02)	0.66	(0.01)	0.08	(0.02)	0.32	(0.02)
Austria	0.06	(0.02)	0.27	(0.01)	0.24	(0.02)	0.01	(0.02)	0.02	(0.02)	0.03	(0.02)	0.01	(0.02)	-0.07	(0.02)	0.04	(0.02)	0.27	(0.01)	0.06	(0.02)	0.10	(0.02)
Belgium (Fl.)	0.20	(0.03)	0.40	(0.02)	0.36	(0.02)	0.00	(0.02)	0.03	(0.02)	0.23	(0.02)	0.07	(0.02)	-0.03	(0.02)	0.12	(0.02)	0.43	(0.02)	0.02	(0.02)	0.20	(0.02)
Czech Republic	0.08	(0.02)	0.32	(0.02)	0.33	(0.02)	0.07	(0.02)	-0.02	(0.02)	0.1	(0.02)	0.04	(0.02)	-0.09	(0.02)	0.02	(0.02)	0.40	(0.02)	0.05	(0.02)	0.14	(0.02)
Denmark	0.56	(0.01)	0.63	(0.01)	0.43	(0.01)	0.15	(0.02)	0.24	(0.02)	0.45	(0.02)	0.18	(0.02)	0.18	(0.02)	0.27	(0.02)	0.59	(0.01)	0.02	(0.02)	0.28	(0.02)
Finland	0.50	(0.01)	0.68	(0.01)	0.49	(0.01)	0.18	(0.02)	0.28	(0.02)	0.46	(0.02)	0.25	(0.02)	0.17	(0.02)	0.35	(0.02)	0.60	(0.01)	0.10	(0.02)	0.32	(0.02)
Germany	0.25	(0.02)	0.48	(0.02)	0.38	(0.02)	0.09	(0.02)	0.11	(0.01)	0.21	(0.02)	0.09	(0.02)	0.04	(0.02)	0.18	(0.02)	0.47	(0.02)	0.07	(0.02)	0.23	(0.02)
Hungary	0.47	(0.01)	0.71	(0.01)	0.46	(0.01)	0.21	(0.02)	0.23	(0.02)	0.47	(0.01)	0.26	(0.02)	0.13	(0.02)	0.37	(0.02)	0.67	(0.01)	0.06	(0.02)	0.33	(0.02)
Iceland	0.55	(0.01)	0.65	(0.01)	0.47	(0.01)	0.15	(0.02)	0.31	(0.02)	0.37	(0.02)	0.2	(0.02)	0.15	(0.02)	0.24	(0.02)	0.57	(0.01)	0.04	(0.02)	0.25	(0.02)
Ireland	0.46	(0.02)	0.67	(0.01)	0.47	(0.02)	0.17	(0.02)	0.20	(0.02)	0.41	(0.02)	0.18	(0.02)	0.14	(0.02)	0.31	(0.02)	0.63	(0.01)	0.08	(0.02)	0.18	(0.02)
Italy	0.07	(0.02)	0.19	(0.02)	0.17	(0.02)	0.00	(0.02)	0.04	(0.02)	0.04	(0.02)	-0.04	(0.02)	-0.03	(0.02)	-0.02	(0.02)	0.16	(0.02)	0.05	(0.01)	0.15	(0.02)
Korea	0.37	(0.01)	0.51	(0.01)	0.34	(0.01)	0.13	(0.02)	0.16	(0.02)	0.32	(0.02)	0.20	(0.02)	0.09	(0.02)	0.28	(0.02)	0.42	(0.01)	0.12	(0.02)	0.35	(0.02)
Luxembourg	0.38	(0.02)	0.53	(0.02)	0.43	(0.02)	0.16	(0.02)	0.19	(0.02)	0.33	(0.02)	0.01	(0.02)	0.09	(0.02)	0.26	(0.02)	0.52	(0.02)	0.15	(0.02)	0.24	(0.01)
Mexico	0.40	(0.02)	0.48	(0.02)	0.39	(0.01)	0.16	(0.02)	0.17	(0.02)	0.38	(0.02)	0.14	(0.02)	0.12	(0.02)	0.21	(0.02)	0.46	(0.02)	0.13	(0.02)	0.23	(0.01)
New Zealand	0.53	(0.02)	0.66	(0.01)	0.51	(0.02)	0.15	(0.02)	0.25	(0.02)	0.49	(0.02)	0.15	(0.02)	0.15	(0.02)	0.31	(0.02)	0.62	(0.01)	0.09	(0.02)	0.28	(0.02)
Norway	0.57	(0.01)	0.67	(0.01)	0.45	(0.02)	0.13	(0.02)	0.26	(0.02)	0.42	(0.02)	0.17	(0.02)	0.16	(0.02)	0.28	(0.02)	0.53	(0.01)	0.04	(0.02)	0.30	(0.02)
Portugal	0.25	(0.02)	0.39	(0.02)	0.33	(0.02)	0.07	(0.02)	0.07	(0.02)	0.26	(0.02)	0.08	(0.02)	0.03	(0.02)	0.14	(0.02)	0.35	(0.02)	0.09	(0.02)	0.14	(0.02)
Scotland	0.43	(0.02)	0.59	(0.01)	0.46	(0.02)	0.11	(0.03)	0.23	(0.02)	0.39	(0.02)	0.11	(0.02)	0.13	(0.02)	0.27	(0.03)	0.54	(0.02)	0.07	(0.02)	0.17	(0.03)
Sweden	0.49	(0.01)	0.67	(0.01)	0.47	(0.01)	0.19	(0.02)	0.25	(0.02)	0.49	(0.01)	0.24	(0.02)	0.2	(0.02)	0.38	(0.02)	0.61	(0.01)	0.00	(0.02)	0.32	(0.02)
Switzerland	0.37	(0.02)	0.5	(0.01)	0.40	(0.01)	0.11	(0.02)	0.14	(0.02)	0.31	(0.02)	0.14	(0.02)	0.04	(0.02)	0.20	(0.02)	0.44	(0.02)	0.08	(0.02)	0.21	(0.02)
United States	0.58	(0.02)	0.69	(0.02)	0.51	(0.02)	0.19	(0.02)	0.23	(0.03)	0.5	(0.03)	0.24	(0.03)	0.14	(0.03)	0.31	(0.02)	0.63	(0.02)	0.18	(0.02)	0.28	(0.02)
OECD average	*0.40*		*0.51*		*0.40*		*0.14*		*0.18*		*0.36*		*0.17*		*0.10*		*0.24*		*0.48*		*0.12*		*0.25*	
NON-OECD COUNTRIES																								
Brazil	0.58	(0.02)	0.65	(0.01)	0.41	(0.02)	0.26	(0.02)	0.30	(0.02)	0.56	(0.01)	0.22	(0.02)	0.25	(0.02)	0.35	(0.02)	0.59	(0.02)	0.12	(0.02)	0.20	(0.02)
Latvia	0.47	(0.02)	0.60	(0.02)	0.44	(0.02)	0.24	(0.02)	0.24	(0.02)	0.39	(0.02)	0.18	(0.02)	0.17	(0.02)	0.28	(0.02)	0.59	(0.01)	0.13	(0.02)	0.29	(0.02)
Liechtenstein	0.20	(0.06)	0.45	(0.04)	0.44	(0.06)	0.14	(0.06)	0.12	(0.07)	0.33	(0.06)	0.14	(0.06)	0.13	(0.06)	0.24	(0.06)	0.45	(0.04)	0.11	(0.07)	0.24	(0.06)
Russian Federation	0.51	(0.01)	0.66	(0.01)	0.49	(0.01)	0.26	(0.02)	0.26	(0.01)	0.48	(0.01)	0.25	(0.02)	0.21	(0.02)	0.35	(0.02)	0.61	(0.01)	0.21	(0.01)	0.31	(0.01)
Netherlands[1]	0.36	(0.02)	0.56	(0.02)	0.42	(0.02)	0.15	(0.02)	0.13	(0.03)	0.33	(0.02)	0.11	(0.02)	0.01	(0.03)	0.18	(0.03)	0.56	(0.02)	0.07	(0.03)	0.22	(0.03)

1. Response rate is too low to ensure comparability.

Note: Standardised regressions coefficients printed in bold are significant (p< 0.05).

Table C2.5b
Relationships between elaboration strategies and learner characteristics
(standardised regression coefficients* and standard errors)

		Control strategies		Instrumental motivation		Interest in reading		Interest in mathematics		Self-efficacy		Self-concept in reading		Mathematical self-concept		Academic self-concept		Effort and persistence		Preference for co-operative learning		Preference for competitive learning	
		Index	S.E.	Index	S.E.	Index	S.E.	Index	S.E.	Index	S.E.	Index	S.E.	Index	S.E.	Index	S.E.	Index	S.E.	Index	S.E.	Index	S.E.
OECD COUNTRIES	Australia	**0.68**	(0.01)	**0.56**	(0.02)	**0.25**	(0.02)	**0.33**	(0.02)	**0.60**	(0.02)	**0.25**	(0.02)	**0.23**	(0.02)	**0.38**	(0.02)	**0.64**	(0.01)	**0.08**	(0.02)	**0.36**	(0.02)
	Austria	**0.50**	(0.01)	**0.30**	(0.02)	**0.16**	(0.02)	**0.23**	(0.02)	**0.46**	(0.01)	**0.12**	(0.02)	**0.17**	(0.02)	**0.31**	(0.01)	**0.45**	(0.02)	**0.08**	(0.02)	**0.29**	(0.02)
	Belgium (Fl.)	**0.52**	(0.01)	**0.36**	(0.02)	**0.15**	(0.02)	**0.27**	(0.02)	**0.48**	(0.02)	**0.15**	(0.02)	**0.17**	(0.02)	**0.31**	(0.02)	**0.45**	(0.02)	**0.13**	(0.02)	**0.27**	(0.02)
	Czech Republic	**0.57**	(0.01)	**0.38**	(0.01)	**0.19**	(0.02)	**0.25**	(0.02)	**0.52**	(0.01)	**0.18**	(0.02)	**0.23**	(0.02)	**0.33**	(0.01)	**0.50**	(0.01)	**0.11**	(0.02)	**0.33**	(0.01)
	Denmark	**0.65**	(0.01)	**0.40**	(0.02)	**0.21**	(0.02)	**0.22**	(0.02)	**0.51**	(0.02)	**0.23**	(0.02)	**0.20**	(0.02)	**0.31**	(0.02)	**0.59**	(0.01)	0.03	(0.02)	**0.29**	(0.02)
	Finland	**0.65**	(0.01)	**0.47**	(0.01)	**0.20**	(0.01)	**0.36**	(0.02)	**0.56**	(0.01)	**0.25**	(0.02)	**0.28**	(0.02)	**0.42**	(0.02)	**0.57**	(0.01)	**0.10**	(0.02)	**0.34**	(0.02)
	Germany	**0.54**	(0.01)	**0.35**	(0.02)	**0.20**	(0.02)	**0.27**	(0.02)	**0.49**	(0.01)	**0.17**	(0.02)	**0.20**	(0.02)	**0.34**	(0.02)	**0.47**	(0.02)	**0.11**	(0.02)	**0.36**	(0.02)
	Hungary	**0.58**	(0.01)	**0.32**	(0.02)	**0.21**	(0.02)	**0.31**	(0.02)	**0.52**	(0.02)	**0.19**	(0.02)	**0.24**	(0.02)	**0.36**	(0.02)	**0.53**	(0.01)	**0.17**	(0.02)	**0.34**	(0.02)
	Iceland	**0.65**	(0.01)	**0.48**	(0.01)	**0.24**	(0.02)	**0.37**	(0.02)	**0.51**	(0.01)	**0.25**	(0.02)	**0.27**	(0.02)	**0.36**	(0.02)	**0.56**	(0.01)	**0.05**	(0.02)	**0.32**	(0.02)
	Ireland	**0.61**	(0.01)	**0.47**	(0.02)	**0.25**	(0.02)	**0.30**	(0.02)	**0.56**	(0.01)	**0.18**	(0.02)	**0.21**	(0.01)	**0.35**	(0.02)	**0.58**	(0.01)	**0.12**	(0.02)	**0.25**	(0.02)
	Italy	**0.48**	(0.01)	**0.29**	(0.02)	**0.23**	(0.02)	**0.28**	(0.02)	**0.45**	(0.01)	**0.19**	(0.01)	**0.19**	(0.02)	**0.33**	(0.02)	**0.48**	(0.01)	**0.06**	(0.02)	**0.24**	(0.02)
	Korea	**0.69**	(0.01)	**0.35**	(0.02)	**0.39**	(0.01)	**0.43**	(0.01)	**0.67**	(0.01)	**0.38**	(0.01)	**0.36**	(0.01)	**0.55**	(0.01)	**0.63**	(0.01)	**0.20**	(0.02)	**0.56**	(0.01)
	Luxembourg	**0.64**	(0.01)	**0.44**	(0.02)	**0.26**	(0.02)	**0.31**	(0.02)	**0.57**	(0.02)	**0.13**	(0.02)	**0.19**	(0.02)	**0.38**	(0.02)	**0.57**	(0.02)	**0.18**	(0.02)	**0.31**	(0.02)
	Mexico	**0.68**	(0.01)	**0.54**	(0.01)	**0.31**	(0.02)	**0.31**	(0.01)	**0.64**	(0.01)	**0.27**	(0.02)	**0.29**	(0.01)	**0.40**	(0.01)	**0.63**	(0.01)	**0.15**	(0.02)	**0.33**	(0.02)
	New Zealand	**0.65**	(0.01)	**0.49**	(0.02)	**0.19**	(0.02)	**0.30**	(0.02)	**0.58**	(0.01)	**0.16**	(0.02)	**0.21**	(0.02)	**0.35**	(0.01)	**0.62**	(0.01)	**0.10**	(0.02)	**0.28**	(0.02)
	Norway	**0.70**	(0.01)	**0.49**	(0.02)	**0.21**	(0.02)	**0.33**	(0.02)	**0.57**	(0.01)	**0.25**	(0.02)	**0.28**	(0.02)	**0.42**	(0.02)	**0.59**	(0.01)	**0.08**	(0.02)	**0.37**	(0.02)
	Portugal	**0.63**	(0.01)	**0.37**	(0.01)	**0.26**	(0.02)	**0.32**	(0.02)	**0.61**	(0.01)	**0.24**	(0.02)	**0.24**	(0.02)	**0.39**	(0.01)	**0.59**	(0.01)	**0.06**	(0.02)	**0.18**	(0.02)
	Scotland	**0.55**	(0.02)	**0.42**	(0.02)	**0.15**	(0.03)	**0.28**	(0.02)	**0.54**	(0.02)	**0.15**	(0.02)	**0.21**	(0.02)	**0.34**	(0.03)	**0.51**	(0.02)	**0.10**	(0.02)	**0.25**	(0.02)
	Sweden	**0.65**	(0.01)	**0.39**	(0.02)	**0.28**	(0.02)	**0.30**	(0.02)	**0.59**	(0.01)	**0.27**	(0.02)	**0.28**	(0.02)	**0.42**	(0.02)	**0.56**	(0.01)	0.03	(0.02)	**0.30**	(0.02)
	Switzerland	0.60	(0.01)	**0.38**	(0.02)	**0.20**	(0.02)	**0.25**	(0.02)	**0.52**	(0.01)	**0.16**	(0.02)	**0.15**	(0.02)	**0.31**	(0.02)	**0.51**	(0.02)	**0.09**	(0.02)	**0.26**	(0.02)
	United States	**0.71**	(0.02)	**0.59**	(0.02)	**0.31**	(0.02)	**0.32**	(0.02)	**0.61**	(0.02)	**0.28**	(0.03)	**0.23**	(0.02)	**0.39**	(0.02)	**0.69**	(0.02)	**0.18**	(0.03)	**0.34**	(0.02)
	OECD average	*0.57*		*0.45*		*0.27*		*0.30*		*0.52*		*0.25*		*0.24*		*0.37*		*0.55*		*0.14*		*0.33*	
NON-OECD COUNTRIES	Brazil	**0.73**	(0.01)	**0.55**	(0.02)	**0.32**	(0.02)	**0.36**	(0.02)	**0.66**	(0.01)	**0.24**	(0.02)	**0.28**	(0.02)	**0.39**	(0.02)	**0.70**	(0.01)	**0.12**	(0.02)	**0.24**	(0.02)
	Latvia	**0.57**	(0.01)	**0.43**	(0.02)	**0.22**	(0.02)	**0.26**	(0.02)	**0.50**	(0.01)	**0.18**	(0.02)	**0.23**	(0.02)	**0.32**	(0.02)	**0.54**	(0.01)	**0.17**	(0.02)	**0.31**	(0.02)
	Liechtenstein	**0.65**	(0.03)	**0.50**	(0.04)	**0.19**	(0.06)	**0.21**	(0.06)	**0.54**	(0.05)	**0.28**	(0.06)	**0.12**	(0.06)	**0.40**	(0.05)	**0.55**	(0.04)	**0.18**	(0.06)	**0.35**	(0.06)
	Russian Federation	**0.64**	(0.01)	**0.48**	(0.01)	**0.29**	(0.01)	**0.31**	(0.01)	**0.58**	(0.01)	**0.23**	(0.02)	**0.27**	(0.01)	**0.38**	(0.01)	**0.62**	(0.01)	**0.26**	(0.01)	**0.36**	(0.01)
	Netherlands[1]	**0.56**	(0.02)	**0.36**	(0.02)	**0.18**	(0.03)	**0.25**	(0.02)	**0.48**	(0.02)	**0.10**	(0.02)	**0.12**	(0.02)	**0.27**	(0.02)	**0.45**	(0.02)	**0.07**	(0.02)	**0.29**	(0.02)

1. Response rate is too low to ensure comparability.
Note: Standardised regressions coefficients printed in bold are significant (p< 0.05).

Table C2.5c
Relationships between control strategies and learner characteristics
(standardised regression coefficients* and standard errors)

		Instrumental motivation		Interest in reading		Interest in mathematics		Self-efficacy		Self-concept in reading		Mathematical self-concept		Academic self-concept		Effort and persistence		Preference for co-operative learning		Preference for competitive learning	
		Index	S.E.	Index	S.E.	Index	S.E.	Index	S.E.	Index	S.E.	Index	S.E.	Index	S.E.	Index	S.E.	Index	S.E.	Index	S.E.
OECD COUNTRIES	Australia	**0.54**	(0.02)	**0.29**	(0.02)	**0.36**	(0.02)	**0.65**	(0.01)	**0.31**	(0.02)	**0.31**	(0.02)	**0.46**	(0.02)	**0.78**	(0.01)	**0.06**	(0.02)	**0.36**	(0.02)
	Austria	**0.39**	(0.02)	**0.20**	(0.02)	**0.20**	(0.01)	**0.46**	(0.01)	**0.21**	(0.02)	**0.15**	(0.02)	**0.39**	(0.01)	**0.61**	(0.01)	**0.08**	(0.02)	**0.29**	(0.02)
	Belgium (Fl.)	**0.44**	(0.02)	**0.21**	(0.02)	**0.24**	(0.02)	**0.51**	(0.01)	**0.20**	(0.02)	**0.12**	(0.02)	**0.36**	(0.02)	**0.68**	(0.01)	**0.07**	(0.02)	**0.24**	(0.02)
	Czech Republic	**0.48**	(0.01)	**0.28**	(0.01)	**0.19**	(0.02)	**0.45**	(0.02)	**0.27**	(0.02)	**0.15**	(0.02)	**0.37**	(0.01)	**0.65**	(0.01)	**0.11**	(0.02)	**0.34**	(0.02)
	Denmark	**0.43**	(0.01)	**0.25**	(0.02)	**0.25**	(0.02)	**0.50**	(0.01)	**0.26**	(0.01)	**0.18**	(0.02)	**0.31**	(0.02)	**0.70**	(0.01)	-0.01	(0.02)	**0.27**	(0.02)
	Finland	**0.53**	(0.01)	**0.26**	(0.02)	**0.38**	(0.01)	**0.57**	(0.01)	**0.33**	(0.01)	**0.27**	(0.02)	**0.46**	(0.01)	**0.71**	(0.01)	**0.09**	(0.02)	**0.33**	(0.02)
	Germany	**0.46**	(0.02)	**0.24**	(0.01)	**0.26**	(0.02)	**0.49**	(0.01)	**0.23**	(0.01)	**0.18**	(0.02)	**0.39**	(0.02)	**0.70**	(0.01)	**0.09**	(0.02)	**0.35**	(0.02)
	Hungary	**0.41**	(0.02)	**0.26**	(0.02)	**0.31**	(0.02)	**0.50**	(0.01)	**0.26**	(0.02)	**0.18**	(0.02)	**0.38**	(0.02)	**0.66**	(0.01)	**0.12**	(0.02)	**0.37**	(0.02)
	Iceland	**0.52**	(0.02)	**0.25**	(0.02)	**0.38**	(0.02)	**0.50**	(0.02)	**0.31**	(0.02)	**0.26**	(0.02)	**0.39**	(0.02)	**0.69**	(0.01)	**0.02**	(0.02)	**0.30**	(0.02)
	Ireland	**0.52**	(0.01)	**0.32**	(0.02)	**0.30**	(0.02)	**0.56**	(0.01)	**0.23**	(0.02)	**0.22**	(0.02)	**0.43**	(0.01)	**0.74**	(0.01)	**0.07**	(0.02)	**0.22**	(0.02)
	Italy	**0.34**	(0.02)	**0.26**	(0.02)	**0.29**	(0.02)	**0.45**	(0.02)	**0.32**	(0.02)	**0.20**	(0.02)	**0.44**	(0.02)	**0.70**	(0.01)	**0.10**	(0.02)	**0.25**	(0.02)
	Korea	**0.39**	(0.02)	**0.34**	(0.01)	**0.43**	(0.01)	**0.63**	(0.01)	**0.37**	(0.01)	**0.33**	(0.02)	**0.55**	(0.01)	**0.71**	(0.01)	**0.18**	(0.02)	**0.56**	(0.01)
	Luxembourg	**0.55**	(0.02)	**0.28**	(0.02)	**0.24**	(0.02)	**0.58**	(0.01)	**0.21**	(0.02)	**0.17**	(0.02)	**0.43**	(0.02)	**0.74**	(0.01)	**0.13**	(0.02)	**0.28**	(0.02)
	Mexico	**0.56**	(0.01)	**0.31**	(0.02)	**0.30**	(0.02)	**0.65**	(0.01)	**0.29**	(0.02)	**0.26**	(0.02)	**0.41**	(0.02)	**0.71**	(0.01)	**0.15**	(0.02)	**0.33**	(0.02)
	New Zealand	**0.52**	(0.02)	**0.26**	(0.02)	**0.32**	(0.02)	**0.63**	(0.01)	**0.22**	(0.02)	**0.26**	(0.02)	**0.44**	(0.01)	**0.75**	(0.01)	**0.07**	(0.02)	**0.31**	(0.02)
	Norway	**0.56**	(0.02)	**0.21**	(0.02)	**0.35**	(0.01)	**0.58**	(0.02)	**0.26**	(0.01)	**0.25**	(0.02)	**0.42**	(0.02)	**0.69**	(0.01)	**0.10**	(0.02)	**0.38**	(0.02)
	Portugal	**0.46**	(0.02)	**0.33**	(0.02)	**0.28**	(0.02)	**0.57**	(0.01)	**0.32**	(0.02)	**0.20**	(0.02)	**0.42**	(0.01)	**0.72**	(0.01)	**0.07**	(0.02)	**0.11**	(0.02)
	Scotland	**0.50**	(0.02)	**0.26**	(0.02)	**0.26**	(0.02)	**0.52**	(0.02)	**0.23**	(0.02)	**0.23**	(0.02)	**0.41**	(0.02)	**0.71**	(0.01)	**0.05**	(0.02)	**0.19**	(0.03)
	Sweden	**0.53**	(0.01)	**0.32**	(0.01)	**0.30**	(0.02)	**0.61**	(0.01)	**0.36**	(0.01)	**0.26**	(0.01)	**0.51**	(0.01)	**0.72**	(0.01)	-0.03	(0.02)	**0.34**	(0.02)
	Switzerland	**0.45**	(0.02)	**0.25**	(0.02)	**0.21**	(0.02)	**0.54**	(0.01)	**0.23**	(0.02)	**0.13**	(0.02)	**0.38**	(0.01)	**0.69**	(0.01)	**0.06**	(0.02)	**0.22**	(0.02)
	United States	**0.57**	(0.02)	**0.32**	(0.02)	**0.32**	(0.02)	**0.65**	(0.02)	**0.36**	(0.03)	**0.25**	(0.02)	**0.48**	(0.02)	**0.80**	(0.01)	**0.20**	(0.03)	**0.34**	(0.03)
	OECD average	*0.47*		*0.29*		*0.30*		*0.54*		*0.31*		*0.24*		*0.42*		*0.63*		*0.15*		*0.33*	
NON-OECD COUNTRIES	Brazil	**0.59**	(0.02)	**0.32**	(0.02)	**0.38**	(0.02)	**0.66**	(0.01)	**0.29**	(0.02)	**0.29**	(0.02)	**0.41**	(0.02)	**0.77**	(0.01)	**0.11**	(0.02)	**0.22**	(0.02)
	Latvia	**0.49**	(0.02)	**0.31**	(0.02)	**0.25**	(0.02)	**0.46**	(0.02)	**0.26**	(0.02)	**0.17**	(0.02)	**0.35**	(0.02)	**0.63**	(0.01)	**0.14**	(0.02)	**0.33**	(0.02)
	Liechtenstein	**0.56**	(0.04)	**0.24**	(0.07)	**0.19**	(0.06)	**0.62**	(0.04)	**0.42**	(0.05)	0.12	(0.07)	**0.52**	(0.04)	**0.74**	(0.03)	**0.15**	(0.07)	**0.40**	(0.06)
	Russian Federation	**0.55**	(0.01)	**0.33**	(0.01)	**0.31**	(0.01)	**0.57**	(0.01)	**0.31**	(0.02)	**0.28**	(0.01)	**0.42**	(0.01)	**0.69**	(0.01)	**0.23**	(0.01)	**0.37**	(0.01)
	Netherlands[1]	**0.45**	(0.02)	**0.24**	(0.02)	**0.22**	(0.02)	**0.49**	(0.02)	**0.18**	(0.02)	0.04	(0.03)	**0.32**	(0.03)	**0.68**	(0.01)	**0.10**	(0.03)	**0.23**	(0.02)

1. Response rate is too low to ensure comparability.
**Note:* Standardised regressions coefficients printed in bold are significant (p< 0.05).

Table C2.5d
Relationships between instrumental motivation and learner characteristics
(standardised regression coefficients* and standard errors)

		Interest in reading		Interest in mathematics		Self-efficacy		Self-concept in reading		Mathematical self-concept		Academic self-concept		Effort and persistence		Preference for co-operative learning		Preference for competitive learning	
		Index	S.E.	Index	S.E.	Index	S.E.	Index	S.E.	Index	S.E.	Index	S.E.	Index	S.E.	Index	S.E.	Index	S.E.
OECD COUNTRIES	Australia	**0.14**	(0.02)	**0.30**	(0.02)	**0.47**	(0.02)	**0.20**	(0.02)	**0.20**	(0.02)	**0.29**	(0.02)	**0.58**	(0.02)	**0.05**	(0.02)	**0.32**	(0.02)
	Austria	-0.01	(0.02)	**0.19**	(0.02)	**0.26**	(0.01)	**0.05**	(0.02)	**0.10**	(0.02)	**0.19**	(0.02)	**0.46**	(0.02)	**0.07**	(0.02)	**0.23**	(0.02)
	Belgium (Fl.)	-0.01	(0.02)	**0.17**	(0.02)	**0.33**	(0.02)	**0.09**	(0.02)	**0.09**	(0.02)	**0.25**	(0.02)	**0.52**	(0.01)	**0.03**	(0.02)	**0.27**	(0.02)
	Czech Republic	**0.09**	(0.02)	**0.16**	(0.02)	**0.31**	(0.02)	**0.15**	(0.02)	**0.12**	(0.01)	**0.25**	(0.01)	**0.52**	(0.01)	**0.11**	(0.02)	**0.33**	(0.02)
	Denmark	0.03	(0.02)	**0.19**	(0.02)	**0.32**	(0.02)	**0.11**	(0.02)	**0.13**	(0.02)	**0.19**	(0.02)	**0.43**	(0.02)	**0.03**	(0.02)	**0.26**	(0.02)
	Finland	**0.18**	(0.01)	**0.33**	(0.02)	**0.47**	(0.01)	**0.29**	(0.01)	**0.28**	(0.02)	**0.42**	(0.02)	**0.58**	(0.01)	**0.07**	(0.02)	**0.35**	(0.02)
	Germany	0.02	(0.02)	**0.21**	(0.02)	**0.30**	(0.02)	**0.10**	(0.02)	**0.12**	(0.02)	**0.23**	(0.02)	**0.51**	(0.01)	**0.08**	(0.02)	**0.31**	(0.02)
	Hungary	0.03	(0.02)	**0.19**	(0.02)	**0.31**	(0.02)	**0.13**	(0.02)	**0.08**	(0.02)	**0.25**	(0.02)	**0.44**	(0.02)	**0.10**	(0.02)	**0.30**	(0.02)
	Iceland	**0.16**	(0.02)	**0.32**	(0.02)	**0.37**	(0.02)	**0.21**	(0.02)	**0.19**	(0.02)	**0.29**	(0.02)	**0.54**	(0.02)	**0.02**	(0.02)	**0.30**	(0.02)
	Ireland	**0.16**	(0.02)	**0.24**	(0.02)	**0.41**	(0.01)	**0.15**	(0.02)	**0.13**	(0.02)	**0.28**	(0.02)	**0.54**	(0.01)	**0.07**	(0.02)	**0.28**	(0.02)
	Italy	**0.02**	(0.02)	**0.22**	(0.02)	**0.28**	(0.02)	**0.07**	(0.02)	**0.11**	(0.02)	**0.20**	(0.02)	**0.37**	(0.02)	**0.07**	(0.02)	**0.26**	(0.02)
	Korea	**0.14**	(0.02)	**0.20**	(0.01)	**0.28**	(0.01)	**0.20**	(0.02)	**0.14**	(0.02)	**0.29**	(0.02)	**0.36**	(0.02)	**0.13**	(0.02)	**0.39**	(0.01)
	Luxembourg	**0.11**	(0.02)	**0.17**	(0.02)	**0.42**	(0.02)	**0.15**	(0.02)	**0.12**	(0.02)	**0.29**	(0.02)	**0.58**	(0.02)	**0.10**	(0.02)	**0.26**	(0.02)
	Mexico	**0.22**	(0.02)	**0.27**	(0.02)	**0.54**	(0.01)	**0.24**	(0.02)	**0.23**	(0.02)	**0.35**	(0.02)	**0.59**	(0.01)	**0.15**	(0.02)	**0.35**	(0.02)
	New Zealand	**0.12**	(0.02)	**0.26**	(0.02)	**0.41**	(0.02)	**0.11**	(0.02)	**0.13**	(0.02)	**0.25**	(0.02)	**0.59**	(0.02)	**0.07**	(0.02)	**0.26**	(0.02)
	Norway	**0.20**	(0.02)	**0.27**	(0.02)	**0.48**	(0.02)	**0.27**	(0.02)	**0.22**	(0.02)	**0.41**	(0.02)	**0.60**	(0.01)	**0.11**	(0.02)	**0.37**	(0.02)
	Portugal	**0.13**	(0.02)	**0.17**	(0.02)	**0.33**	(0.02)	**0.16**	(0.02)	**0.09**	(0.02)	**0.22**	(0.02)	**0.44**	(0.02)	**0.09**	(0.02)	**0.18**	(0.02)
	Scotland	**0.15**	(0.02)	**0.21**	(0.02)	**0.41**	(0.02)	**0.12**	(0.03)	**0.18**	(0.02)	**0.31**	(0.02)	**0.51**	(0.02)	**0.06**	(0.02)	**0.21**	(0.02)
	Sweden	**0.17**	(0.02)	**0.25**	(0.01)	**0.39**	(0.01)	**0.23**	(0.02)	**0.19**	(0.01)	**0.34**	(0.02)	**0.55**	(0.01)	0.00	(0.02)	**0.31**	(0.02)
	Switzerland	**0.06**	(0.02)	**0.20**	(0.02)	**0.32**	(0.02)	**0.11**	(0.02)	**0.10**	(0.02)	**0.21**	(0.02)	**0.50**	(0.02)	**0.09**	(0.02)	**0.25**	(0.02)
	United States	**0.23**	(0.02)	**0.29**	(0.02)	**0.47**	(0.02)	**0.20**	(0.03)	**0.19**	(0.02)	**0.3**	(0.02)	**0.61**	(0.02)	**0.14**	(0.02)	**0.30**	(0.02)
	OECD average	*0.16*		*0.25*		*0.39*		*0.18*		*0.17*		*0.28*		*0.49*		*0.12*		*0.3*	
NON-OECD COUNTRIES	Brazil	**0.17**	(0.02)	**0.27**	(0.02)	**0.47**	(0.02)	**0.19**	(0.02)	**0.17**	(0.02)	**0.22**	(0.02)	**0.63**	(0.02)	**0.07**	(0.02)	**0.14**	(0.02)
	Latvia	**0.20**	(0.02)	**0.21**	(0.02)	**0.42**	(0.02)	**0.26**	(0.02)	**0.17**	(0.02)	**0.34**	(0.02)	**0.51**	(0.01)	**0.07**	(0.02)	**0.33**	(0.02)
	Liechtenstein	0.08	(0.06)	**0.25**	(0.06)	**0.43**	(0.06)	**0.30**	(0.05)	0.17	(0.06)	**0.38**	(0.04)	**0.67**	(0.03)	0.18	(0.07)	**0.35**	(0.06)
	Russian Federation	**0.21**	(0.02)	**0.27**	(0.01)	**0.46**	(0.01)	**0.27**	(0.02)	**0.25**	(0.02)	**0.39**	(0.02)	**0.56**	(0.01)	**0.17**	(0.01)	**0.34**	(0.01)
	Netherlands[1]	0.00	(0.03)	**0.21**	(0.02)	**0.39**	(0.03)	0.06	(0.02)	0.05	(0.03)	**0.21**	(0.03)	**0.48**	(0.02)	**0.07**	(0.02)	**0.27**	(0.02)

1. Response rate is too low to ensure comparability.
**Note:* Standardised regressions coefficients printed in bold are significant (p< 0.05).

Table C2.5e
Relationships between interest in reading and learner characteristics
(standardised regression coefficients* and standard errors)

		Interest in mathematics		Self-efficacy		Self-concept in reading		Mathematical self-concept		Academic self-concept		Effort and persistence		Preference for co-operative learning		Preference for competitive learning	
		Index	S.E.	Index	S.E.	Index	S.E.	Index	S.E.	Index	S.E.	Index	S.E.	Index	S.E.	Index	S.E.
OECD COUNTRIES	Australia	0.12	(0.02)	0.23	(0.02)	0.31	(0.02)	0.10	(0.02)	0.26	(0.02)	0.27	(0.02)	-0.04	(0.02)	0.19	(0.02)
	Austria	-0.04	(0.02)	0.10	(0.02)	0.24	(0.02)	-0.05	(0.02)	0.19	(0.02)	0.14	(0.02)	0.06	(0.02)	0.09	(0.02)
	Belgium (Fl.)	0.10	(0.02)	0.14	(0.02)	0.21	(0.02)	0.00	(0.02)	0.13	(0.02)	0.16	(0.02)	0.09	(0.02)	0.09	(0.02)
	Czech Republic	0.04	(0.02)	0.11	(0.01)	0.26	(0.02)	0.04	(0.02)	0.21	(0.02)	0.19	(0.01)	0.13	(0.02)	0.16	(0.02)
	Denmark	0.08	(0.02)	0.19	(0.02)	0.33	(0.02)	0.05	(0.02)	0.28	(0.02)	0.29	(0.02)	-0.03	(0.02)	0.18	(0.02)
	Finland	0.11	(0.01)	0.18	(0.01)	0.37	(0.01)	0.07	(0.02)	0.30	(0.01)	0.31	(0.01)	0.03	(0.02)	0.11	(0.01)
	Germany	0.02	(0.02)	0.18	(0.02)	0.32	(0.01)	-0.03	(0.02)	0.20	(0.02)	0.22	(0.02)	0.08	(0.02)	0.13	(0.02)
	Hungary	0.14	(0.02)	0.15	(0.02)	0.28	(0.02)	0.10	(0.02)	0.22	(0.02)	0.22	(0.02)	0.12	(0.02)	0.25	(0.02)
	Iceland	0.22	(0.02)	0.23	(0.02)	0.26	(0.02)	0.14	(0.02)	0.31	(0.02)	0.27	(0.02)	0.02	(0.02)	0.20	(0.02)
	Ireland	0.12	(0.02)	0.26	(0.02)	0.24	(0.02)	0.10	(0.02)	0.29	(0.02)	0.26	(0.02)	0.09	(0.02)	0.14	(0.02)
	Italy	0.07	(0.02)	0.16	(0.02)	0.27	(0.01)	0.01	(0.02)	0.18	(0.02)	0.24	(0.02)	0.09	(0.02)	0.07	(0.02)
	Korea	0.21	(0.02)	0.34	(0.01)	0.36	(0.01)	0.15	(0.02)	0.32	(0.01)	0.30	(0.01)	0.15	(0.01)	0.31	(0.02)
	Luxembourg	0.13	(0.02)	0.19	(0.02)	0.14	(0.02)	0.07	(0.02)	0.24	(0.02)	0.24	(0.02)	0.26	(0.02)	0.22	(0.02)
	Mexico	0.30	(0.02)	0.28	(0.02)	0.27	(0.02)	0.22	(0.02)	0.31	(0.02)	0.31	(0.02)	0.20	(0.02)	0.24	(0.02)
	New Zealand	0.14	(0.02)	0.23	(0.02)	0.28	(0.02)	0.14	(0.02)	0.33	(0.02)	0.23	(0.02)	0.01	(0.02)	0.18	(0.02)
	Norway	0.18	(0.02)	0.24	(0.02)	0.36	(0.02)	0.15	(0.02)	0.35	(0.02)	0.30	(0.02)	0.03	(0.02)	0.20	(0.02)
	Portugal	0.17	(0.02)	0.20	(0.02)	0.34	(0.02)	0.07	(0.02)	0.25	(0.02)	0.29	(0.02)	0.15	(0.02)	0.05	(0.02)
	Scotland	0.06	(0.03)	0.20	(0.02)	0.24	(0.02)	0.06	(0.03)	0.22	(0.02)	0.23	(0.02)	0.01	(0.02)	0.10	(0.02)
	Sweden	0.17	(0.01)	0.30	(0.02)	0.36	(0.02)	0.15	(0.02)	0.35	(0.02)	0.34	(0.02)	-0.06	(0.02)	0.21	(0.02)
	Switzerland	-0.07	(0.02)	0.18	(0.02)	0.28	(0.02)	-0.12	(0.02)	0.17	(0.02)	0.21	(0.02)	0.07	(0.02)	0.03	(0.02)
	United States	0.16	(0.03)	0.34	(0.02)	0.32	(0.02)	0.14	(0.02)	0.36	(0.02)	0.34	(0.02)	0.05	(0.02)	0.23	(0.03)
	OECD average	*0.15*		*0.27*		*0.30*		*0.11*		*0.29*		*0.29*		*0.08*		*0.20*	
NON-OECD COUNTRIES	Brazil	0.27	(0.02)	0.27	(0.02)	0.31	(0.02)	0.18	(0.02)	0.36	(0.02)	0.31	(0.02)	0.20	(0.02)	0.19	(0.02)
	Latvia	0.15	(0.02)	0.23	(0.02)	0.34	(0.02)	0.07	(0.02)	0.30	(0.02)	0.29	(0.02)	0.17	(0.02)	0.25	(0.02)
	Liechtenstein	0.02	(0.05)	0.24	(0.06)	0.22	(0.06)	0.05	(0.06)	0.22	(0.07)	0.22	(0.06)	-0.01	(0.06)	0.17	(0.06)
	Russian Federation	0.25	(0.01)	0.26	(0.01)	0.34	(0.01)	0.22	(0.01)	0.32	(0.01)	0.34	(0.01)	0.27	(0.01)	0.28	(0.01)
	Netherlands[1]	0.03	(0.03)	0.12	(0.02)	0.19	(0.02)	-0.08	(0.03)	0.16	(0.02)	0.20	(0.03)	0.06	(0.02)	0.06	(0.02)

1. Response rate is too low to ensure comparability.

*Note: Standardised regressions coefficients printed in bold are significant (p< 0.05).

Table C2.5f
**Relationships between interest in mathematics and learner characteristics
(standardised regression coefficients* and standard errors)**

	Self-efficacy		Self-concept in reading		Mathematical self-cncept		Academic self-concept		Effort and persistence		Preference for co-operative learning		Preference for competitive learning	
	Index	S.E.	Index	S.E.	Index	S.E.	Index	S.E.	Index	S.E.	Index	S.E.	Index	S.E.
Australia	0.38	(0.02)	0.00	(0.02)	0.66	(0.01)	0.36	(0.02)	0.40	(0.02)	0.02	(0.02)	0.37	(0.02)
Austria	0.28	(0.01)	-0.13	(0.02)	0.67	(0.01)	0.22	(0.02)	0.28	(0.02)	0.02	(0.02)	0.26	(0.02)
Belgium (Fl.)	0.30	(0.02)	-0.06	(0.02)	0.65	(0.01)	0.28	(0.02)	0.26	(0.02)	0.05	(0.02)	0.28	(0.02)
Czech Republic	0.31	(0.02)	-0.02	(0.02)	0.67	(0.01)	0.31	(0.02)	0.24	(0.02)	0.14	(0.02)	0.29	(0.01)
Denmark	0.30	(0.02)	-0.03	(0.02)	0.75	(0.01)	0.36	(0.02)	0.30	(0.02)	0.04	(0.02)	0.36	(0.02)
Finland	0.46	(0.01)	0.16	(0.02)	0.74	(0.01)	0.47	(0.01)	0.44	(0.01)	0.07	(0.02)	0.38	(0.02)
Germany	0.33	(0.01)	-0.11	(0.02)	0.71	(0.01)	0.33	(0.01)	0.30	(0.02)	0.05	(0.02)	0.32	(0.02)
Hungary	0.35	(0.02)	0.03	(0.02)	0.70	(0.01)	0.32	(0.02)	0.33	(0.02)	0.18	(0.02)	0.36	(0.02)
Iceland	0.44	(0.01)	0.19	(0.02)	0.58	(0.01)	0.38	(0.02)	0.42	(0.02)	0.01	(0.02)	0.36	(0.02)
Ireland	0.37	(0.02)	-0.04	(0.02)	0.65	(0.01)	0.30	(0.02)	0.31	(0.02)	0.10	(0.02)	0.24	(0.02)
Italy	0.27	(0.02)	-0.02	(0.02)	0.67	(0.01)	0.32	(0.02)	0.35	(0.02)	0.06	(0.02)	0.23	(0.01)
Korea	0.49	(0.01)	0.10	(0.02)	0.82	(0.01)	0.48	(0.01)	0.49	(0.01)	0.19	(0.02)	0.48	(0.02)
Luxembourg	0.32	(0.02)	-0.08	(0.02)	0.66	(0.01)	0.35	(0.02)	0.28	(0.02)	0.22	(0.02)	0.38	(0.02)
Mexico	0.32	(0.02)	0.17	(0.02)	0.60	(0.01)	0.41	(0.02)	0.35	(0.01)	0.16	(0.02)	0.33	(0.02)
New Zealand	0.36	(0.02)	-0.10	(0.02)	0.65	(0.01)	0.38	(0.02)	0.35	(0.02)	0.09	(0.02)	0.38	(0.02)
Norway	0.38	(0.01)	0.04	(0.02)	0.71	(0.01)	0.40	(0.02)	0.36	(0.02)	0.05	(0.02)	0.42	(0.02)
Portugal	0.29	(0.02)	0.06	(0.02)	0.65	(0.01)	0.33	(0.02)	0.31	(0.01)	0.10	(0.02)	0.21	(0.02)
Scotland	0.31	(0.02)	-0.07	(0.03)	0.66	(0.02)	0.29	(0.02)	0.28	(0.02)	0.06	(0.02)	0.26	(0.03)
Sweden	0.33	(0.02)	0.07	(0.02)	0.70	(0.01)	0.37	(0.02)	0.39	(0.02)	0.02	(0.02)	0.33	(0.02)
Switzerland	0.28	(0.02)	-0.18	(0.02)	0.70	(0.01)	0.27	(0.02)	0.27	(0.01)	0.06	(0.02)	0.36	(0.02)
United States	0.36	(0.02)	0.04	(0.03)	0.70	(0.01)	0.39	(0.02)	0.36	(0.02)	0.13	(0.02)	0.34	(0.02)
OECD average	*0.34*		*0.03*		*0.60*		*0.36*		*0.34*		*0.11*		*0.32*	
Brazil	0.40	(0.02)	0.13	(0.02)	0.65	(0.01)	0.48	(0.02)	0.38	(0.02)	0.17	(0.02)	0.32	(0.02)
Latvia	0.27	(0.02)	0.09	(0.02)	0.64	(0.01)	0.39	(0.02)	0.35	(0.02)	0.25	(0.03)	0.29	(0.02)
Liechtenstein	0.24	(0.07)	-0.07	(0.06)	0.67	(0.04)	0.31	(0.07)	0.25	(0.06)	0.19	(0.06)	0.38	(0.06)
Russian Federation	0.38	(0.02)	0.14	(0.02)	0.74	(0.01)	0.46	(0.02)	0.40	(0.01)	0.24	(0.01)	0.37	(0.01)
Netherlands[1]	0.29	(0.02)	-0.02	(0.02)	0.67	(0.01)	0.29	(0.02)	0.24	(0.03)	0.11	(0.02)	0.28	(0.02)

OECD COUNTRIES / NON-OECD COUNTRIES

1. Response rate is too low to ensure comparability.
*Note: Standardised regressions coefficients printed in bold are significant (p< 0.05).

Table C2.5g
**Relationships between self-efficacy and learner characteristics
(standardised regression coefficients* and standard errors)**

		Self-concept in reading		Mathematical self-concept		Academic self-concept		Effort and persistence		Preference for co-operative learning		Preference for competitive learning	
		Index	S.E.	Index	S.E.	Index	S.E.	Index	S.E.	Index	S.E.	Index	S.E.
OECD COUNTRIES	Australia	**0.37**	(0.02)	**0.43**	(0.02)	**0.59**	(0.01)	**0.64**	(0.01)	0.03	(0.02)	**0.41**	(0.02)
	Austria	**0.21**	(0.02)	**0.33**	(0.02)	**0.52**	(0.01)	**0.47**	(0.02)	-0.03	(0.02)	**0.30**	(0.02)
	Belgium (Fl.)	**0.26**	(0.02)	**0.31**	(0.02)	**0.55**	(0.01)	**0.50**	(0.02)	0.04	(0.02)	**0.30**	(0.02)
	Czech Republic	**0.27**	(0.02)	**0.38**	(0.02)	**0.49**	(0.02)	**0.49**	(0.02)	0.03	(0.02)	**0.39**	(0.01)
	Denmark	**0.36**	(0.02)	**0.39**	(0.01)	**0.60**	(0.01)	**0.55**	(0.01)	**-0.10**	(0.02)	**0.38**	(0.02)
	Finland	**0.39**	(0.01)	**0.50**	(0.01)	**0.66**	(0.01)	**0.60**	(0.01)	0.03	(0.02)	**0.43**	(0.02)
	Germany	0.24	(0.02)	**0.37**	(0.02)	**0.58**	(0.01)	**0.51**	(0.01)	0.03	(0.02)	**0.43**	(0.01)
	Hungary	**0.25**	(0.02)	**0.37**	(0.02)	**0.52**	(0.01)	**0.56**	(0.01)	**0.10**	(0.02)	**0.38**	(0.02)
	Iceland	**0.46**	(0.02)	**0.52**	(0.01)	**0.66**	(0.01)	**0.52**	(0.02)	-0.01	(0.02)	**0.44**	(0.02)
	Ireland	**0.25**	(0.02)	**0.38**	(0.02)	**0.56**	(0.01)	**0.56**	(0.01)	0.04	(0.02)	**0.36**	(0.02)
	Italy	**0.29**	(0.01)	**0.26**	(0.02)	**0.50**	(0.02)	**0.47**	(0.02)	-0.03	(0.02)	**0.27**	(0.02)
	Korea	**0.38**	(0.01)	**0.44**	(0.02)	**0.64**	(0.01)	**0.63**	(0.01)	**0.18**	(0.02)	**0.59**	(0.01)
	Luxembourg	**0.26**	(0.02)	**0.30**	(0.02)	**0.54**	(0.02)	**0.57**	(0.01)	**0.10**	(0.02)	**0.38**	(0.02)
	Mexico	**0.30**	(0.02)	**0.32**	(0.02)	**0.48**	(0.01)	**0.63**	(0.01)	**0.11**	(0.02)	**0.35**	(0.02)
	New Zealand	**0.25**	(0.02)	**0.40**	(0.02)	**0.58**	(0.01)	**0.61**	(0.01)	**0.05**	(0.02)	**0.47**	(0.01)
	Norway	**0.38**	(0.02)	**0.45**	(0.01)	**0.65**	(0.01)	**0.59**	(0.01)	0.02	(0.02)	**0.47**	(0.01)
	Portugal	0.32	(0.02)	**0.29**	(0.02)	**0.51**	(0.01)	**0.53**	(0.01)	0.01	(0.02)	**0.20**	(0.01)
	Scotland	**0.22**	(0.03)	**0.40**	(0.02)	**0.53**	(0.02)	**0.54**	(0.02)	0.07	(0.03)	**0.33**	(0.02)
	Sweden	**0.43**	(0.01)	**0.44**	(0.01)	**0.66**	(0.01)	**0.56**	(0.01)	**-0.07**	(0.02)	**0.38**	(0.02)
	Switzerland	**0.26**	(0.02)	**0.28**	(0.02)	**0.51**	(0.01)	**0.52**	(0.01)	0.00	(0.02)	**0.31**	(0.01)
	United States	**0.37**	(0.02)	**0.39**	(0.02)	**0.60**	(0.01)	**0.64**	(0.02)	0.07	(0.03)	**0.41**	(0.02)
	OECD average	*0.32*		*0.36*		*0.52*		*0.53*		*0.06*		*0.38*	
NON-OECD COUNTRIES	Brazil	**0.26**	(0.02)	**0.38**	(0.02)	**0.49**	(0.01)	**0.64**	(0.01)	**0.06**	(0.02)	**0.27**	(0.02)
	Latvia	**0.29**	(0.02)	**0.32**	(0.02)	**0.50**	(0.01)	**0.51**	(0.01)	**0.11**	(0.02)	**0.34**	(0.02)
	Liechtenstein	**0.45**	(0.05)	**0.28**	(0.06)	**0.57**	(0.04)	**0.65**	(0.04)	0.14	(0.07)	**0.43**	(0.06)
	Russian Federation	**0.30**	(0.02)	**0.43**	(0.01)	**0.56**	(0.01)	**0.61**	(0.01)	**0.20**	(0.01)	**0.40**	(0.01)
	Netherlands[1]	**0.23**	(0.02)	**0.24**	(0.02)	**0.50**	(0.02)	**0.45**	(0.02)	**0.05**	(0.02)	**0.31**	(0.02)

1. Response rate is too low to ensure comparability.
**Note:* Standardised regressions coefficients printed in bold are significant (p< 0.05).

Table C2.5h
Relationships between self-concept in reading and learner characteristics
(standardised regresssion coefficients* and standard errors)

	Mathematical self-concept		Academic self-concept		Effort and persistence		Preference for co-operative learning		Preference for competitive learning	
	Index	S.E.	Index	S.E.	Index	S.E.	Index	S.E.	Index	S.E.
OECD COUNTRIES										
Australia	0.01	(0.02)	**0.46**	(0.02)	**0.28**	(0.02)	**0.07**	(0.02)	**0.24**	(0.02)
Austria	**-0.08**	(0.02)	**0.37**	(0.02)	**0.14**	(0.02)	0.01	(0.02)	**0.17**	(0.02)
Belgium (Fl.)	**-0.10**	(0.02)	**0.31**	(0.02)	**0.16**	(0.02)	**0.05**	(0.02)	**0.13**	(0.02)
Czech Republic	0.03	(0.02)	**0.43**	(0.01)	**0.23**	(0.02)	**0.06**	(0.02)	**0.26**	(0.02)
Denmark	0.02	(0.02)	**0.52**	(0.01)	**0.30**	(0.02)	0.00	(0.02)	**0.24**	(0.02)
Finland	**0.22**	(0.02)	**0.54**	(0.01)	**0.39**	(0.01)	**0.07**	(0.02)	**0.25**	(0.02)
Germany	**-0.14**	(0.02)	**0.34**	(0.02)	**0.20**	(0.02)	**0.08**	(0.02)	**0.22**	(0.01)
Hungary	**0.06**	(0.02)	**0.41**	(0.02)	**0.25**	(0.02)	**0.06**	(0.02)	**0.24**	(0.02)
Iceland	**0.24**	(0.02)	**0.60**	(0.01)	**0.36**	(0.02)	-0.01	(0.02)	**0.29**	(0.02)
Ireland	**-0.09**	(0.02)	**0.34**	(0.02)	**0.22**	(0.02)	**0.09**	(0.02)	**0.13**	(0.02)
Italy	**-0.08**	(0.02)	**0.40**	(0.01)	**0.28**	(0.02)	**0.04**	(0.02)	**0.14**	(0.02)
Korea	0.03	(0.02)	**0.42**	(0.02)	**0.33**	(0.02)	**0.12**	(0.02)	**0.37**	(0.02)
Luxembourg	-0.02	(0.02)	**0.33**	(0.02)	**0.19**	(0.02)	0.00	(0.02)	**0.09**	(0.02)
Mexico	**0.19**	(0.02)	**0.41**	(0.02)	**0.30**	(0.02)	**0.12**	(0.02)	**0.25**	(0.02)
New Zealand	**-0.08**	(0.02)	**0.34**	(0.02)	**0.20**	(0.02)	**0.08**	(0.02)	**0.12**	(0.02)
Norway	**0.11**	(0.02)	**0.54**	(0.01)	**0.35**	(0.02)	**0.06**	(0.02)	**0.26**	(0.02)
Portugal	0.02	(0.02)	**0.43**	(0.02)	**0.28**	(0.02)	**0.04**	(0.02)	**0.06**	(0.02)
Scotland	**-0.08**	(0.03)	**0.28**	(0.02)	**0.18**	(0.02)	**0.07**	(0.03)	**0.08**	(0.02)
Sweden	**0.14**	(0.02)	**0.54**	(0.01)	**0.35**	(0.02)	-0.04	(0.02)	**0.21**	(0.02)
Switzerland	**-0.19**	(0.02)	**0.33**	(0.02)	**0.18**	(0.02)	**0.04**	(0.02)	**0.05**	(0.02)
United States	0.05	(0.03)	**0.46**	(0.03)	**0.35**	(0.03)	**0.10**	(0.02)	**0.25**	(0.03)
OECD average	*0.03*		*0.40*		*0.29*		*0.09*		*0.23*	
NON-OECD COUNTRIES										
Brazil	**0.08**	(0.03)	**0.36**	(0.03)	**0.27**	(0.02)	**0.08**	(0.02)	**0.11**	(0.02)
Latvia	**0.04**	(0.02)	**0.41**	(0.02)	**0.26**	(0.02)	**0.15**	(0.02)	**0.30**	(0.02)
Liechtenstein	-0.11	(0.06)	**0.42**	(0.05)	**0.34**	(0.05)	**0.23**	(0.07)	**0.23**	(0.08)
Russian Federation	**0.20**	(0.01)	**0.46**	(0.01)	**0.33**	(0.02)	**0.18**	(0.02)	**0.33**	(0.01)
Netherlands[1]	**-0.05**	(0.02)	**0.32**	(0.02)	**0.18**	(0.02)	**0.08**	(0.02)	**0.09**	(0.02)

1. Response rate is too low to ensure comparability.
**Note:* Standardised regressions coefficients printed in bold are significant (p< 0.05).

Table C2.5i
Relationships between mathematical self-concept and learner characteristics
(standardised regression coefficients* and standard errors)

	Academic self-concept		Effort and persistence		Preference for co-operative learning		Preference for competitive learning	
	Index	S.E.	Index	S.E.	Index	S.E.	Index	S.E.
Australia	0.51	(0.01)	0.31	(0.02)	0.02	(0.03)	0.36	(0.02)
Austria	0.40	(0.02)	0.21	(0.02)	-0.03	(0.02)	0.24	(0.02)
Belgium (Fl.)	0.36	(0.02)	0.16	(0.02)	0.04	(0.02)	0.25	(0.02)
Czech Republic	0.43	(0.01)	0.19	(0.02)	0.07	(0.02)	0.30	(0.01)
Denmark	0.49	(0.01)	0.23	(0.02)	0.01	(0.02)	0.36	(0.02)
Finland	0.58	(0.01)	0.34	(0.01)	-0.02	(0.02)	0.37	(0.02)
Germany	0.43	(0.02)	0.21	(0.02)	0.01	(0.02)	0.30	(0.02)
Hungary	0.42	(0.02)	0.24	(0.02)	0.10	(0.02)	0.30	(0.02)
Iceland	0.53	(0.01)	0.31	(0.02)	0.00	(0.02)	0.36	(0.02)
Ireland	0.34	(0.01)	0.23	(0.02)	0.05	(0.02)	0.23	(0.02)
Italy	0.39	(0.01)	0.26	(0.02)	-0.01	(0.02)	0.18	(0.02)
Korea	0.49	(0.01)	0.39	(0.02)	0.15	(0.02)	0.41	(0.02)
Luxembourg	0.40	(0.02)	0.20	(0.02)	0.16	(0.02)	0.33	(0.02)
Mexico	0.52	(0.02)	0.34	(0.01)	0.10	(0.02)	0.27	(0.02)
New Zealand	0.54	(0.01)	0.24	(0.02)	0.06	(0.02)	0.38	(0.02)
Norway	0.53	(0.01)	0.31	(0.02)	0.00	(0.02)	0.41	(0.02)
Portugal	0.40	(0.02)	0.22	(0.02)	0.01	(0.02)	0.21	(0.02)
Scotland	0.42	(0.02)	0.24	(0.02)	0.07	(0.02)	0.27	(0.03)
Sweden	0.50	(0.01)	0.31	(0.02)	-0.03	(0.02)	0.32	(0.01)
Switzerland	0.37	(0.02)	0.17	(0.02)	0.02	(0.02)	0.30	(0.02)
United States	0.49	(0.02)	0.29	(0.02)	0.09	(0.02)	0.34	(0.02)
OECD average	0.44		0.28		0.07		0.30	
Brazil	0.52	(0.02)	0.29	(0.02)	0.06	(0.02)	0.31	(0.02)
Latvia	0.43	(0.02)	0.28	(0.02)	0.10	(0.03)	0.27	(0.02)
Liechtenstein	0.38	(0.06)	0.24	(0.07)	0.11	(0.07)	0.32	(0.07)
Russian Federation	0.61	(0.01)	0.37	(0.01)	0.19	(0.02)	0.38	(0.01)
Netherlands[1]	0.34	(0.02)	0.07	(0.03)	0.05	(0.02)	0.20	(0.02)

1. Response rate is too low to ensure comparability.
**Note:* Standardised regressions coefficients printed in bold are significant (p< 0.05).

Table C2.5j
Relationships between learner characteristics (standardised regression coefficients* and standard errors)

| | Correlation between academic self-concept and the learner characteristics below | | | | | | Correlation between effort and persistence and the learner characteristics below | | | | Correlation between preference for co-operative learning and preference for competitive learning | |
| | Effort and persistence | | Preference for co-operative learning | | Preference for competitive learning | | Preference for co-operative learning | | Preference for competitive learning | | | |
	Index	S.E.	Index	S.E.	Index	S.E.	Index	S.E.	Index	S.E.	Index	S.E.
OECD COUNTRIES												
Australia	0.43	(0.02)	0.09	(0.03)	0.44	(0.02)	0.05	(0.02)	0.33	(0.02)	0.02	(0.02)
Austria	0.41	(0.01)	0.00	(0.02)	0.37	(0.02)	0.04	(0.02)	0.30	(0.02)	0.01	(0.02)
Belgium (Fl.)	0.38	(0.02)	0.07	(0.03)	0.33	(0.02)	0.05	(0.02)	0.27	(0.02)	0.08	(0.02)
Czech Republic	0.36	(0.01)	0.13	(0.02)	0.46	(0.01)	0.09	(0.02)	0.36	(0.01)	0.13	(0.02)
Denmark	0.37	(0.02)	-0.01	(0.02)	0.45	(0.02)	-0.02	(0.02)	0.29	(0.02)	0.01	(0.02)
Finland	0.54	(0.01)	0.06	(0.02)	0.48	(0.01)	0.11	(0.02)	0.33	(0.02)	0.02	(0.02)
Germany	0.42	(0.02)	0.08	(0.02)	0.48	(0.02)	0.06	(0.02)	0.35	(0.02)	0.10	(0.02)
Hungary	0.44	(0.02)	0.11	(0.02)	0.43	(0.02)	0.09	(0.02)	0.36	(0.02)	0.18	(0.02)
Iceland	0.45	(0.02)	0.07	(0.02)	0.42	(0.02)	0.00	(0.02)	0.27	(0.02)	0.08	(0.02)
Ireland	0.45	(0.02)	0.13	(0.02)	0.33	(0.02)	0.07	(0.02)	0.20	(0.02)	0.02	(0.02)
Italy	0.46	(0.02)	0.02	(0.02)	0.30	(0.02)	0.09	(0.02)	0.26	(0.02)	0.01	(0.02)
Korea	0.56	(0.01)	0.21	(0.01)	0.58	(0.01)	0.23	(0.02)	0.58	(0.01)	0.26	(0.02)
Luxembourg	0.44	(0.02)	0.21	(0.02)	0.45	(0.02)	0.14	(0.02)	0.32	(0.02)	0.22	(0.02)
Mexico	0.43	(0.01)	0.21	(0.02)	0.40	(0.02)	0.13	(0.02)	0.33	(0.02)	0.18	(0.02)
New Zealand	0.42	(0.02)	0.15	(0.02)	0.44	(0.02)	0.09	(0.02)	0.28	(0.02)	0.09	(0.02)
Norway	0.50	(0.01)	0.09	(0.02)	0.54	(0.01)	0.07	(0.02)	0.37	(0.02)	0.05	(0.02)
Portugal	0.40	(0.02)	0.08	(0.02)	0.27	(0.02)	0.09	(0.02)	0.12	(0.02)	0.08	(0.02)
Scotland	0.40	(0.02)	0.16	(0.03)	0.30	(0.02)	0.09	(0.02)	0.16	(0.02)	0.08	(0.02)
Sweden	0.51	(0.01)	-0.03	(0.02)	0.41	(0.02)	-0.01	(0.02)	0.32	(0.02)	-0.02	(0.02)
Switzerland	0.39	(0.02)	0.06	(0.02)	0.36	(0.02)	0.04	(0.02)	0.28	(0.02)	0.10	(0.02)
United States	0.47	(0.02)	0.19	(0.03)	0.45	(0.02)	0.20	(0.02)	0.31	(0.02)	0.15	(0.02)
OECD average	*0.43*		*0.15*		*0.41*		*0.14*		*0.32*		*0.13*	
NON-OECD COUNTRIES												
Brazil	0.40	(0.02)	0.15	(0.02)	0.37	(0.02)	0.10	(0.02)	0.22	(0.02)	0.19	(0.02)
Latvia	0.41	(0.02)	0.22	(0.02)	0.46	(0.02)	0.15	(0.02)	0.36	(0.02)	0.22	(0.03)
Liechtenstein	0.55	(0.04)	0.25	(0.07)	0.43	(0.06)	0.14	(0.07)	0.39	(0.06)	0.17	(0.07)
Russian Federation	0.49	(0.01)	0.26	(0.02)	0.47	(0.01)	0.25	(0.01)	0.40	(0.01)	0.30	(0.02)
Netherlands[1]	0.31	(0.03)	0.09	(0.03)	0.34	(0.02)	0.08	(0.02)	0.21	(0.03)	0.13	(0.03)

1. Response rate is too low to ensure comparability.
Note: Standardised regressions coefficients printed in bold are significant (p< 0.05).

Table C2.6
Predicting the use of control strategies: Combined effects of interest in reading, instrumental motivation and self-efficacy[1]

		Interest in reading	Self-efficacy	Instrumental motivation
OECD COUNTRIES	Australia	0.12	0.60	0.31
	Austria	0.19	0.53	0.35
	Belgium (Fl.)	0.18	0.56	0.32
	Czech Republic	0.25	0.41	0.40
	Denmark	0.20	0.47	0.38
	Finland	0.15	0.49	0.37
	Germany	0.21	0.48	0.40
	Hungary	0.20	0.50	0.31
	Iceland	0.13	0.42	0.46
	Ireland	0.16	0.48	0.37
	Italy	0.21	0.46	0.26
	Korea	0.10	0.74	0.24
	Luxembourg	0.17	0.50	0.41
	Mexico	0.09	0.61	0.29
	New Zealand	0.10	0.60	0.32
	Norway	0.07	0.48	0.43
	Portugal	0.20	0.58	0.31
	Scotland	0.14	0.43	0.41
	Sweden	0.15	0.54	0.36
	Switzerland	0.15	0.56	0.33
	United States	0.07	0.57	0.35
NON-OECD COUNTRIES	Brazil	0.09	0.66	0.31
	Latvia	0.17	0.38	0.44
	Liechtenstein	0.06	0.63	0.35
	Russian Federation	0.17	0.46	0.42
	Netherlands[2]	0.23	0.46	0.37

1. Standardised regression coefficients of the structural equation model.

2. Response rate is too low to ensure comparability.

Table C2.7a
**Predicting reading literacy: Combined direct effects[1] of interest reading, instrumental motivation,
self-efficacy and the use of control strategies**

		Instrumental motivation	Interest in reading	Self-efficacy	Control strategies
OECD COUNTRIES	Australia	-0.19	0.31	0.07	0.26
	Austria	-0.22	0.31	0.13	0.21
	Belgium (Fl.)	-0.18	0.27	0.08	0.14
	Czech Republic	-0.19	0.29	0.05	0.34
	Denmark	-0.03	0.31	0.46	-0.20
	Finland	0.13	0.45	0.33	-0.26
	Germany	-0.25	0.30	0.10	0.27
	Hungary	-0.05	0.32	0.09	0.05
	Iceland	0.02	0.37	0.47	-0.25
	Ireland	-0.14	0.33	0.13	0.12
	Italy	-0.20	0.21	0.05	0.22
	Korea	0.03	0.23	0.10	0.16
	Luxembourg	-0.04	0.16	0.05	0.21
	Mexico	-0.03	-0.07	0.00	0.34
	New Zealand	-0.26	0.28	-0.06	0.45
	Norway	0.19	0.36	0.53	-0.49
	Portugal	-0.07	0.12	-0.02	0.44
	Scotland	-0.05	0.37	0.11	0.12
	Sweden	-0.06	0.36	0.31	-0.09
	Switzerland	-0.19	0.29	0.12	0.19
	United States	-0.35	0.20	0.26	0.19
NON-OECD COUNTRIES	Brazil	0.11	-0.03	0.07	0.23
	Latvia	0.27	0.29	0.18	-0.21
	Liechtenstein	-0.22	0.27	0.18	0.17
	Russian Federation	0.14	0.18	0.16	-0.03
	Netherlands[2]	-0.21	0.28	0.17	0.07

1. Standardised regression coefficients of the structural equation model.
2. Response rate is too low to ensure comparability.

Table C2.7b
**Predicting reading literacy: Total effects[1] of interest in reading,
instrumental motivation, self-efficacy and the use of control strategies**

		Instrumental motivation	Interest in reading	Self-efficacy	Control strategies	
OECD COUNTRIES	Australia	-0.11	0.34	0.23	0.26	(0.26)[2]
	Austria	-0.14	0.35	0.22	0.21	(0.20)
	Belgium (Fl.)	-0.13	0.29	0.16	0.14	(0.13)
	Czech Republic	-0.05	0.37	0.19	0.34	(0.31)
	Denmark	-0.10	0.26	0.36	-0.20	(0.15)
	Finland	0.04	0.41	0.20	-0.26	(0.15)
	Germany	-0.14	0.36	0.22	0.27	(0.24)
	Hungary	-0.03	0.33	0.11	0.05	(0.15)
	Iceland	-0.10	0.33	0.36	-0.25	(0.15)
	Ireland	-0.10	0.35	0.19	0.12	(0.22)
	Italy	-0.14	0.25	0.15	0.22	(0.19)
	Korea	0.06	0.25	0.22	0.16	(0.30)
	Luxembourg	0.05	0.20	0.15	0.21	(0.25)
	Mexico	0.07	-0.04	0.21	0.34	(0.24)
	New Zealand	-0.12	0.32	0.22	0.45	(0.28)
	Norway	-0.02	0.32	0.30	-0.49	(0.11)
	Portugal	0.07	0.21	0.23	0.44	(0.37)
	Scotland	0.00	0.39	0.17	0.12	(0.24)
	Sweden	-0.10	0.34	0.26	-0.09	(0.19)
	Switzerland	-0.13	0.32	0.23	0.19	(0.22)
	United States	-0.28	0.21	0.37	0.19	(0.20)
NON-OECD COUNTRIES	Brazil	0.18	-0.01	0.22	0.23	(0.27)
	Latvia	0.17	0.26	0.11	-0.21	(0.18)
	Liechtenstein	-0.16	0.28	0.29	0.17	(0.22)
	Russian Federation	0.12	0.17	0.15	-0.03	(0.23)
	Netherlands[3]	-0.19	0.29	0.20	0.07	(0.10)

1. Standardised regression coefficients of the structural equation model.
2. Bivariate effects of control strategies on reading literacy presented in parenthesis.
3. Response rate is too low to ensure comparability.

Table C2.8
**Unique and common contributions of the learner characteristics scales
and student socio-economic background in predicting reading literacy**

		Unique effects (%)					Total (%)	
		Interest in reading	Self-efficacy	Control strategies	Instrumental motivation	Socio-economic background[1]	Shared variance[2]	Explained variance
OECD COUNTRIES	Australia	6	0	1	1	6	12	26
	Austria	6	0	2	1	6	12	27
	Belgium (Fl.)	5	0	0	1	9	8	23
	Czech Republic	5	0	4	1	8	14	32
	Denmark	7	7	1	0	3	9	27
	Finland	17	4	2	1	2	4	30
	Germany	6	1	3	3	8	11	32
	Hungary	7	0	0	0	11	6	24
	Iceland	11	10	2	0	0	7	30
	Ireland	8	1	1	2	7	7	26
	Italy	3	0	3	2	6	5	19
	Korea	4	0	0	0	1	14	19
	Luxembourg	2	0	1	0	14	7	24
	Mexico	0	0	2	0	12	5	19
	New Zealand	6	0	4	3	5	9	27
	Norway	10	9	6	1	1	7	34
	Portugal	2	1	5	1	11	11	31
	Scotland	9	0	0	0	8	12	29
	Sweden	9	3	0	0	3	11	26
	Switzerland	6	0	1	1	9	10	27
	United States	3	2	1	5	9	6	26
NON-OECD COUNTRIES	Brazil	0	3	0	1	9	10	23
	Latvia	7	1	1	3	3	6	21
	Liechtenstein	5	0	1	2	11	10	29
	Russian Federation	3	1	0	1	7	6	18
	Netherlands[3]	5	1	0	1	8	8	23

1. Measured by the International Socio-Economic Index of Occupational Status of mother or father, whichever is higher.

2. Reported for the whole country.

3. Response rate is too low to ensure comparability.

Table C3.1a
Country-level means for learner characteristics scales where cross-level bias is likely

		Elaboration strategies		Instrumental motivation		Interest in reading		Interest in mathematics		Effort and persistence		Preference for competitive learning		Academic self-concept		Control strategies	
		Index	S.E.	Index	S.E.	Index	S.E.	Index	S.E.	Index	S.E.	Index	S.E.	Index	S.E.	Index	S.E.
OECD COUNTRIES	Australia	2.56	(0.01)	2.71	(0.02)	2.56	(0.02)	2.51	(0.01)	2.74	(0.02)	2.72	(0.02)	2.92	(0.02)	2.74	(0.01)
	Austria	2.62	(0.01)	3.07	(0.02)	2.47	(0.03)	2.24	(0.02)	2.85	(0.01)	2.51	(0.01)	2.80	(0.02)	2.99	(0.01)
	Belgium (Fl.)	2.40	(0.01)	2.91	(0.02)	2.27	(0.02)	2.33	(0.02)	2.76	(0.01)	2.34	(0.01)	2.79	(0.02)	2.82	(0.02)
	Czech Republic	2.57	(0.01)	2.97	(0.02)	2.66	(0.02)	2.38	(0.02)	2.64	(0.01)	2.70	(0.01)	2.75	(0.01)	2.91	(0.01)
	Denmark	2.43	(0.01)	2.83	(0.01)	2.73	(0.02)	2.83	(0.02)	2.70	(0.01)	2.81	(0.01)	3.12	(0.01)	2.58	(0.01)
	Finland	2.40	(0.01)	2.89	(0.01)	2.73	(0.02)	2.38	(0.02)	2.71	(0.01)	2.39	(0.01)	2.79	(0.01)	2.42	(0.01)
	Germany	2.55	(0.01)	2.95	(0.01)	2.50	(0.02)	2.39	(0.02)	2.78	(0.01)	2.61	(0.02)	2.79	(0.01)	2.89	(0.01)
	Hungary	2.62	(0.01)	3.27	(0.02)	2.49	(0.02)	2.39	(0.02)	2.89	(0.01)	2.66	(0.01)	2.67	(0.01)	2.87	(0.02)
	Iceland	2.35	(0.01)	2.93	(0.02)	2.51	(0.02)	2.54	(0.01)	2.67	(0.01)	2.58	(0.02)	2.80	(0.01)	2.50	(0.01)
	Ireland	2.45	(0.01)	2.80	(0.02)	2.59	(0.02)	2.45	(0.02)	2.71	(0.01)	2.63	(0.02)	3.12	(0.01)	2.78	(0.01)
	Italy	2.44	(0.01)	2.80	(0.02)	2.46	(0.03)	2.45	(0.02)	2.76	(0.02)	2.63	(0.02)	2.93	(0.01)	2.88	(0.01)
	Korea	2.50	(0.02)	2.54	(0.01)	2.25	(0.02)	2.20	(0.02)	2.47	(0.02)	2.48	(0.02)	2.12	(0.02)	2.45	(0.01)
	Luxembourg	2.43	(0.01)	3.00	(0.02)	2.49	(0.02)	2.28	(0.02)	2.71	(0.01)	2.51	(0.02)	2.78	(0.02)	2.76	(0.01)
	Mexico	2.73	(0.01)	2.97	(0.02)	2.74	(0.01)	2.81	(0.01)	2.85	(0.01)	3.09	(0.01)	2.87	(0.01)	2.83	(0.01)
	New Zealand	2.57	(0.01)	2.72	(0.02)	2.63	(0.02)	2.53	(0.02)	2.71	(0.01)	2.79	(0.02)	2.97	(0.01)	2.78	(0.01)
	Norway	2.37	(0.01)	2.84	(0.02)	2.57	(0.02)	2.23	(0.02)	2.63	(0.01)	2.55	(0.02)	2.85	(0.01)	2.36	(0.02)
	Portugal	2.61	(0.01)	3.13	(0.02)	2.78	(0.02)	2.69	(0.01)	2.83	(0.01)	2.43	(0.02)	2.82	(0.02)	2.85	(0.01)
	Scotland	2.64	(0.01)	3.03	(0.02)	2.50	(0.03)	2.47	(0.02)	2.92	(0.02)	2.68	(0.02)	3.15	(0.01)	2.95	(0.01)
	Sweden	2.52	(0.01)	3.15	(0.01)	2.67	(0.01)	2.28	(0.01)	2.74	(0.01)	2.55	(0.01)	2.91	(0.02)	2.76	(0.01)
	Switzerland	2.57	(0.01)	2.86	(0.02)	2.60	(0.02)	2.41	(0.02)	2.74	(0.01)	2.48	(0.01)	2.82	(0.01)	2.81	(0.01)
	United States	2.52	(0.02)	2.55	(0.02)	2.58	(0.03)	2.51	(0.02)	2.67	(0.02)	2.79	(0.02)	3.08	(0.02)	2.69	(0.02)
	OECD average	*2.51*	*(0.08)*	*2.89*	*(0.03)*	*2.57*	*(0.01)*	*2.44*	*(0.00)*	*2.73*	*(0.00)*	*2.62*	*(0.00)*	*2.84*	*(0.00)*	*2.73*	*(0.01)*
NON-OECD COUNTRIES	Brazil	2.84	(0.02)	3.25	(0.02)	2.88	(0.02)	3.04	(0.02)	3.00	(0.02)	2.56	(0.02)	2.92	(0.01)	2.87	(0.02)
	Latvia	2.53	(0.01)	2.95	(0.02)	2.79	(0.02)	2.79	(0.03)	2.55	(0.01)	2.82	(0.02)	2.85	(0.02)	2.66	(0.01)
	Liechtenstein	2.51	(0.04)	2.84	(0.04)	2.48	(0.05)	2.39	(0.05)	2.79	(0.04)	2.55	(0.04)	2.87	(0.03)	2.82	(0.03)
	Russian Federation	2.60	(0.01)	3.23	(0.01)	2.70	(0.02)	2.56	(0.02)	2.70	(0.01)	2.72	(0.01)	2.74	(0.02)	2.79	(0.01)
	Netherlands[1]	2.38	(0.01)	2.84	(0.02)	2.40	(0.04)	2.45	(0.02)	2.62	(0.01)	2.44	(0.02)	3.01	(0.02)	2.69	(0.01)

1. Response rate is too low to ensure comparability.

Table C3.1b
Performance on the combined reading literacy scale[1]

		Total		Males		Females	
		Mean	S.E.	Mean	S.E.	Mean	S.E.
OECD COUNTRIES	Australia	528	(3.5)	513	(4.0)	546	(4.7)
	Austria	507	(2.4)	495	(3.2)	520	(3.6)
	Belgium (Fl.)	532	(4.3)	492	(4.2)	525	(4.9)
	Czech Republic	492	(2.4)	473	(4.1)	510	(2.5)
	Denmark	497	(2.4)	485	(3.0)	510	(2.9)
	Finland	546	(2.6)	520	(3.0)	571	(2.8)
	Germany	484	(2.5)	468	(3.2)	502	(3.9)
	Hungary	480	(4.0)	465	(5.3)	496	(4.3)
	Iceland	507	(1.5)	488	(2.1)	528	(2.1)
	Ireland	527	(3.2)	513	(4.2)	542	(3.6)
	Italy	487	(2.9)	469	(5.1)	507	(3.6)
	Korea	525	(2.4)	519	(3.8)	533	(3.7)
	Luxembourg	441	(1.6)	429	(2.6)	456	(2.3)
	Mexico	422	(3.3)	411	(4.2)	432	(3.8)
	New Zealand	529	(2.8)	507	(4.2)	553	(3.8)
	Norway	505	(2.8)	486	(3.8)	529	(2.9)
	Portugal	470	(4.5)	458	(5.0)	482	(4.6)
	United Kingdom[2]	523	(2.6)	512	(3.0)	537	(3.4)
	Sweden	516	(2.2)	499	(2.6)	536	(2.5)
	Switzerland	494	(4.3)	480	(4.9)	510	(4.5)
	United States	504	(7.1)	490	(8.4)	518	(6.2)
	OECD average	*500*	*(0.7)*	*485*	*(0.8)*	*517*	*(0.7)*
NON-OECD COUNTRIES	Brazil	396	(3.1)	388	(3.9)	404	(3.4)
	Latvia	458	(5.3)	432	(5.5)	485	(5.4)
	Liechtenstein	483	(4.1)	468	(7.3)	500	(6.8)
	Russian Federation	462	(4.2)	443	(4.5)	481	(4.1)

1. The reading literacy scale has a mean (OECD average) of 500 and a standard deviation of 100.
2. Performance on the combined reading literacy scale was computed for the United Kingdom.

Table C3.2
Country means and standard deviations for a selection of learner characteristics scales[1]

		Memorisation strategies			Self-concept in reading			Mathematical self-concept			Self-efficacy			Preference for co-operative learning		
		Index	S.E.	S.D.	Index	S.E.	S.D.	Index	S.E.	S.D.	Index	S.E.	S.D.	Index	S.E.	S.D.
OECD COUNTRIES	Australia	2.59	(0.01)	0.64	2.93	(0.01)	0.58	2.60	(0.02)	0.77	2.62	(0.02)	0.62	2.86	(0.01)	0.57
	Austria	2.47	(0.01)	0.70	2.94	(0.01)	0.76	2.39	(0.02)	0.92	2.67	(0.01)	0.63	2.57	(0.02)	0.78
	Belgium (Fl.)	2.52	(0.01)	0.72	2.82	(0.01)	0.60	2.43	(0.02)	0.79	2.60	(0.01)	0.59	2.55	(0.01)	0.60
	Czech Republic	2.44	(0.01)	0.68	2.72	(0.01)	0.74	2.32	(0.02)	0.88	2.41	(0.01)	0.57	2.65	(0.01)	0.68
	Denmark	2.51	(0.01)	0.56	3.18	(0.01)	0.69	2.91	(0.02)	0.93	2.52	(0.01)	0.64	2.99	(0.01)	0.67
	Finland	2.40	(0.01)	0.57	2.88	(0.03)	0.70	2.42	(0.05)	1.00	2.47	(0.01)	0.63	2.81	(0.01)	0.64
	Germany	2.51	(0.01)	0.70	2.84	(0.02)	0.77	2.48	(0.02)	0.95	2.59	(0.01)	0.61	2.56	(0.01)	0.74
	Hungary	3.14	(0.01)	0.57	2.82	(0.01)	0.71	2.15	(0.02)	0.91	2.58	(0.01)	0.59	2.11	(0.02)	0.81
	Iceland	2.29	(0.01)	0.62	2.88	(0.02)	0.74	2.47	(0.02)	0.99	2.58	(0.01)	0.72	2.46	(0.01)	0.75
	Ireland	2.69	(0.01)	0.70	3.10	(0.02)	0.77	2.42	(0.02)	0.96	2.50	(0.01)	0.70	2.74	(0.02)	0.83
	Italy	2.00	(0.02)	0.61	3.11	(0.01)	0.77	2.48	(0.02)	1.00	2.59	(0.01)	0.61	2.78	(0.02)	0.79
	Korea	2.37	(0.01)	0.65	2.67	(0.02)	0.67	1.99	(0.02)	0.95	2.28	(0.01)	0.67	2.27	(0.01)	0.74
	Luxembourg	2.44	(0.01)	0.75	3.02	(0.01)	0.76	2.42	(0.02)	0.93	2.49	(0.02)	0.65	2.41	(0.02)	0.78
	Mexico	2.53	(0.01)	0.68	2.96	(0.01)	0.57	2.59	(0.02)	0.76	2.76	(0.01)	0.63	2.92	(0.02)	0.67
	New Zealand	2.66	(0.02)	0.64	2.83	(0.01)	0.78	2.62	(0.02)	0.97	2.60	(0.02)	0.61	2.95	(0.01)	0.69
	Norway	2.08	(0.01)	0.65	2.89	(0.02)	0.75	2.38	(0.02)	1.00	2.56	(0.01)	0.67	2.95	(0.02)	0.78
	Portugal	2.50	(0.01)	0.65	2.88	(0.02)	0.71	2.26	(0.02)	0.96	2.54	(0.01)	0.56	2.98	(0.02)	0.68
	Scotland	2.75	(0.02)	0.62	3.08	(0.02)	0.73	2.61	(0.02)	0.94	2.63	(0.01)	0.61	2.95	(0.02)	0.70
	Sweden	2.61	(0.01)	0.65	2.90	(0.03)	0.61	2.51	(0.03)	0.84	2.65	(0.01)	0.66	2.62	(0.01)	0.64
	Switzerland	2.48	(0.01)	0.64	2.98	(0.02)	0.67	2.37	(0.02)	0.88	2.59	(0.01)	0.56	2.68	(0.01)	0.67
	United States	2.55	(0.02)	0.71	3.08	(0.01)	0.77	2.77	(0.02)	0.93	2.63	(0.02)	0.70	2.99	(0.02)	0.76
	OECD average	*2.49*	*(0.00)*	*0.65*	*2.92*	*(0.00)*	*0.71*	*2.45*	*(0.00)*	*0.92*	*2.56*	*(0.00)*	*0.63*	*2.70*	*(0.00)*	*0.71*
NON-OECD COUNTRIES	Brazil	2.66	(0.02)	0.69	2.92	(0.02)	0.68	2.62	(0.02)	0.90	2.78	(0.01)	0.69	2.87	(0.02)	0.77
	Latvia	2.62	(0.01)	0.54	3.00	(0.01)	0.70	2.49	(0.01)	0.87	2.45	(0.01)	0.55	2.89	(0.03)	0.72
	Liechtenstein	2.41	(0.03)	0.64	2.86	(0.02)	0.67	2.53	(0.02)	0.84	2.60	(0.03)	0.60	2.72	(0.04)	0.66
	Russian Federation	2.76	(0.01)	0.59	2.99	(0.02)	0.74	2.49	(0.03)	0.96	2.52	(0.01)	0.61	2.59	(0.02)	0.76
	Netherlands[2]	2.46	(0.01)	0.58	2.94	(0.01)	0.69	2.44	(0.02)	1.01	2.58	(0.02)	0.56	2.73	(0.01)	0.71

1. Scales range from 1 (low) to 4 (high).
2. Response rate is too low to ensure comparability.

Table C3.3
**Correlation between student mathematical and
self-concept in reading**

		Correlation	S.E.
OECD COUNTRIES	Australia	0.01	(0.02)
	Austria	**-0.08**	(0.02)
	Belgium (Fl.)	-0.10	(0.02)
	Czech Republic	0.03	(0.02)
	Denmark	0.02	(0.02)
	Finland	**0.22**	(0.02)
	Germany	**-0.14**	(0.02)
	Hungary	**0.06**	(0.02)
	Iceland	**0.24**	(0.02)
	Ireland	**-0.09**	(0.02)
	Italy	**-0.08**	(0.02)
	Korea	0.03	(0.02)
	Luxembourg	-0.02	(0.02)
	Mexico	**0.19**	(0.02)
	New Zealand	**-0.08**	(0.02)
	Norway	**0.11**	(0.02)
	Portugal	0.02	(0.02)
	Scotland	**-0.08**	(0.03)
	Sweden	**0.14**	(0.02)
	Switzerland	**-0.19**	(0.02)
	United States	0.05	(0.03)
	OECD average	*0.03*	
NON-OECD COUNTRIES	Brazil	**0.08**	(0.03)
	Latvia	**0.04**	(0.02)
	Liechtenstein	-0.11	(0.06)
	Russian Federation	**0.20**	(0.01)
	Netherlands[1]	**-0.05**	(0.02)

1. The response rate is to low to ensure comparability.
Note: Standardised regressions coefficients printed in bold are significant
(p< 0.05).

Table C3.4
Proportion of between-school variance[1] by scale of learner characteristics

		Memorisation strategies	Elaboration strategies	Control strategies	Instrumental motivation	Interest in reading	Interest in mathematics	Self-efficacy	Self-concept in reading	Mathematical self-concept	Academic self-concept	Effort and persistence	Preference for co-operative learning	Preference for competitive learning
OECD COUNTRIES	Australia	0.07	0.06	0.07	0.06	0.09	0.08	0.07	0.06	0.06	0.05	0.07	0.07	0.07
	Austria	0.08	0.07	0.09	0.08	0.14	0.09	0.08	0.11	0.08	0.06	0.06	0.06	0.06
	Belgium (Fl.)	0.07	0.05	0.08	0.05	0.11	0.08	0.06	0.05	0.07	0.05	0.06	0.06	0.05
	Czech Republic	0.10	0.08	0.12	0.07	0.12	0.09	0.08	0.11	0.09	0.07	0.08	0.08	0.09
	Denmark	0.07	0.08	0.07	0.07	0.07	0.07	0.09	0.08	0.07	0.07	0.07	0.07	0.07
	Finland	0.04	0.05	0.05	0.04	0.05	0.05	0.04	0.06	0.05	0.04	0.05	0.05	0.04
	Germany	0.11	0.08	0.09	0.07	0.13	0.08	0.06	0.07	0.07	0.07	0.06	0.06	0.07
	Hungary	0.14	0.10	0.14	0.11	0.15	0.10	0.11	0.15	0.13	0.13	0.13	0.13	0.09
	Iceland	0.04	0.01	0.02	0.02	0.01	0.03	0.02	0.06	0.03	0.02	0.02	0.02	0.01
	Irland	0.06	0.04	0.07	0.05	0.09	0.04	0.06	0.08	0.04	0.05	0.04	0.04	0.05
	Italy	0.07	0.09	0.14	0.10	0.14	0.12	0.11	0.12	0.08	0.09	0.11	0.11	0.07
	Korea	0.06	0.15	0.12	0.06	0.09	0.16	0.12	0.09	0.11	0.08	0.10	0.10	0.04
	Luxembourg	0.02	0.01	0.04	0.02	0.02	0.01	0.01	0.04	0.00	0.01	0.01	0.01	0.02
	Mexico	0.09	0.09	0.10	0.10	0.08	0.08	0.12	0.11	0.09	0.09	0.08	0.08	0.09
	New Zealand	0.06	0.05	0.08	0.06	0.06	0.07	0.07	0.06	0.07	0.05	0.05	0.05	0.06
	Norway	0.07	0.06	0.07	0.06	0.06	0.06	0.08	0.08	0.07	0.07	0.06	0.06	0.07
	Portugal	0.05	0.06	0.10	0.06	0.05	0.04	0.06	0.09	0.06	0.06	0.06	0.06	0.06
	Scotland	0.05	0.05	0.06	0.05	0.07	0.05	0.06	0.06	0.08	0.06	0.05	0.05	0.05
	Sweden	0.06	0.05	0.06	0.05	0.06	0.06	0.06	0.06	0.05	0.05	0.06	0.06	0.05
	Switzerland	0.12	0.08	0.11	0.07	0.10	0.08	0.08	0.08	0.07	0.08	0.09	0.09	0.08
	United States	0.11	0.10	0.10	0.08	0.08	0.09	0.08	0.12	0.09	0.10	0.09	0.09	0.06
NON-OECD COUNTRIES	Brazil	0.09	0.10	0.11	0.12	0.10	0.09	0.10	0.12	0.10	0.09	0.10	0.10	0.08
	Latvia	0.05	0.05	0.07	0.09	0.07	0.16	0.07	0.09	0.08	0.08	0.05	0.05	0.15
	Liechtenstein	0.01	0.09	0.06	0.00	0.07	0.01	0.07	0.00	0.01	0.01	0.03	0.03	0.02
	Russian Federation	0.08	0.07	0.09	0.08	0.09	0.10	0.09	0.11	0.09	0.10	0.09	0.09	0.08
	Netherlands[2]	0.07	0.05	0.08	0.06	0.10	0.05	0.05	0.09	0.06	0.05	0.07	0.07	0.06

1. The between-school variance by scale of self-regulated learning and country was computed using SPSS's Varcomp (method: ANOVA [Type I Sum of squares]) individually for each country and scale. The numbers in the table are per cent.
2. Response rate is too low to ensure comparability.

Table C3.5
Mean scores on the scales[1] of learner characteristics for the four clusters of learner characteristics

	Strongest learners (Cluster 1)		Stronger learners, weaker in mathematics (Cluster 2)		Weaker learners, stronger in mathematics (Cluster 3)		Weakest learners (Cluster 4)	
	Mean[2]	S.E.	Mean	S.E.	Mean	S.E.	Mean	S.E.
Memorisation strategies	0.65	(0.007)	0.30	(0.006)	-0.33	(0.006)	-0.80	(0.008)
Elaboration strategies	0.90	(0.007)	0.13	(0.006)	-0.27	(0.005)	-0.98	(0.006)
Control strategies	0.95	(0.006)	0.26	(0.005)	-0.34	(0.005)	-1.12	(0.008)
Instrumental motivation	0.69	(0.006)	0.26	(0.007)	-0.25	(0.006)	-0.90	(0.007)
Interest in reading	0.42	(0.007)	0.17	(0.007)	-0.15	(0.007)	-0.54	(0.009)
Interest in mathematics	0.74	(0.007)	-0.63	(0.006)	0.45	(0.005)	-0.80	(0.007)
Self-efficacy	1.02	(0.006)	-0.05	(0.006)	-0.16	(0.005)	-1.05	(0.006)
Self-concept in reading	0.47	(0.007)	0.27	(0.006)	-0.26	(0.006)	-0.58	(0.009)
Mathematical self-concept	0.73	(0.007)	-0.76	(0.004)	0.56	(0.005)	-0.75	(0.007)
Self-concept in reading	0.85	(0.005)	-0.13	(0.006)	0.08	(0.006)	-1.04	(0.008)
Effort and persistence	0.97	(0.005)	0.18	(0.005)	-0.29	(0.005)	-1.11	(0.008)
Preference for co-operative learning	0.12	(0.009)	0.04	(0.008)	0.03	(0.007)	-0.26	(0.011)
Preference for competitive learning	0.67	(0.007)	-0.16	(0.007)	0.08	(0.006)	-0.81	(0.007)

1. The scales have a mean of 0 and a standard deviation of 1 within each country.
2. Mean scores for the OECD countries.

Table C3.6
Percentage and mean reading performance of students by cluster of learner [1]

		Students in cluster								Mean reading performance on the combined reading literacy scale							
		Cluster 1		Cluster 2		Cluster 3		Cluster 4		Cluster 1		Cluster 2		Cluster 3		Cluster 4	
		%	S.E.	%	S.E.	%	S.E.	%	S.E.	%	S.E.	%	S.E.	%	S.E.	%	S.E.
OECD COUNTRIES	Australia	26	(0.97)	26	(0.77)	28	(0.83)	20	(0.82)	569	(4.66)	538	(4.58)	522	(4.08)	499	(4.57)
	Austria	24	(0.73)	30	(0.88)	30	(0.92)	17	(0.68)	533	(3.33)	519	(3.18)	502	(4.05)	490	(4.61)
	Belgium (Fl.)	23	(0.91)	28	(1.03)	32	(0.85)	17	(0.81)	545	(6.18)	550	(3.76)	539	(5.06)	514	(7.30)
	Czech Republic	24	(0.76)	29	(0.79)	30	(0.84)	18	(0.85)	531	(3.42)	511	(3.21)	501	(3.11)	472	(3.41)
	Denmark	26	(0.91)	25	(0.86)	31	(0.89)	18	(0.56)	544	(3.21)	497	(3.08)	511	(3.71)	453	(4.09)
	Finland	28	(0.78)	25	(0.69)	26	(0.71)	21	(0.80)	588	(3.44)	544	(4.05)	547	(3.63)	508	(3.25)
	Germany	25	(0.62)	27	(0.80)	30	(0.79)	17	(0.58)	522	(3.64)	516	(3.48)	493	(3.69)	469	(5.00)
	Hungary	26	(1.03)	28	(0.95)	26	(0.82)	19	(0.78)	508	(5.30)	495	(4.42)	487	(5.37)	450	(4.85)
	Iceland	27	(0.81)	26	(0.81)	27	(0.86)	20	(0.69)	554	(3.11)	501	(3.11)	518	(2.66)	467	(3.43)
	Ireland	26	(0.81)	26	(0.68)	28	(0.76)	19	(0.68)	558	(4.04)	533	(3.44)	527	(4.43)	498	(5.01)
	Italy	24	(0.77)	29	(0.83)	30	(0.81)	17	(0.66)	507	(4.00)	488	(2.94)	494	(3.49)	462	(7.38)
	Korea	27	(1.00)	28	(0.71)	23	(0.70)	22	(0.84)	554	(3.03)	525	(2.59)	528	(3.48)	489	(3.24)
	Luxembourg	26	(0.98)	27	(0.90)	29	(0.82)	18	(0.88)	476	(3.82)	479	(3.12)	448	(3.03)	439	(4.38)
	Mexico	28	(1.09)	24	(0.82)	28	(0.66)	21	(0.86)	447	(5.16)	440	(4.27)	416	(4.11)	400	(3.53)
	Norway	28	(0.87)	26	(0.79)	26	(0.72)	19	(0.76)	559	(3.89)	509	(4.05)	519	(4.00)	463	(4.91)
	New Zealand	27	(0.97)	25	(0.89)	29	(0.86)	19	(0.81)	570	(4.73)	541	(4.17)	536	(3.78)	502	(4.82)
	Portugal	24	(0.87)	27	(0.84)	31	(0.83)	18	(0.80)	511	(4.42)	483	(4.09)	459	(5.92)	427	(5.29)
	Scotland	27	(1.12)	27	(1.01)	27	(0.83)	19	(0.93)	558	(4.62)	528	(5.90)	525	(4.86)	491	(4.98)
	Sweden	27	(0.82)	25	(0.70)	27	(0.87)	21	(0.74)	554	(3.48)	522	(2.90)	513	(3.04)	483	(3.58)
	Switzerland	23	(0.73)	28	(0.88)	32	(0.98)	17	(0.79)	517	(5.46)	525	(4.97)	490	(4.83)	472	(6.13)
	United States	28	(0.93)	24	(0.99)	29	(1.24)	20	(1.03)	543	(7.72)	518	(6.65)	520	(6.69)	469	(8.77)
NON-OECD COUNTRIES	Brazil	29	(1.02)	26	(0.90)	26	(0.96)	19	(0.81)	430	(4.03)	415	(4.05)	397	(4.82)	374	(4.26)
	Latvia	27	(0.93)	24	(1.11)	31	(1.29)	18	(0.88)	495	(6.86)	473	(5.49)	457	(6.37)	421	(5.91)
	Liechtenstein	26	(2.38)	25	(2.62)	28	(2.67)	21	(2.45)	516	(9.43)	503	(8.46)	470	(9.73)	469	(12.00)
	Russian Federation	29	(0.66)	23	(0.67)	25	(0.63)	22	(0.70)	496	(4.80)	472	(4.73)	468	(4.57)	426	(4.81)
	Netherlands [2]	23	(1.04)	29	(1.23)	30	(1.22)	17	(1.10)	538	(5.73)	551	(4.42)	533	(3.41)	515	(7.50)

1. Cluster 1: strongest learners; Cluster 2: stronger learners, weaker in mathematics; Cluster 3: weaker learners, stronger in mathematics; Cluster 4: weakest learners.
2. Response rate is too low to ensure comparability.

Table C3.7
Percentage of males and females students in each cluster of learner[1]

	Cluster 1				Cluster 2				Cluster 3				Cluster 4			
	Females		Males		Females		Males		Females		Males		Females		Males	
OECD COUNTRIES																
Australia	23	(1.2)	33	(1.3)	31	(1.3)	21	(1.0)	22	(1.3)	18	(1.1)	25	(1.5)	28	(1.2)
Austria	24	(1.2)	36	(1.3)	38	(1.3)	21	(1.0)	16	(1.0)	17	(1.0)	22	(0.7)	26	(1.3)
Belgium(Fl.)	28	(1.0)	36	(1.0)	35	(1.3)	22	(1.3)	16	(1.1)	17	(1.0)	21	(1.1)	25	(1.2)
Czech Republic	25	(0.9)	36	(1.5)	36	(1.1)	20	(0.9)	15	(0.9)	20	(1.2)	24	(0.9)	24	(1.1)
Denmark	27	(1.1)	36	(1.3)	30	(1.2)	20	(1.0)	20	(1.0)	15	(0.9)	24	(1.0)	29	(1.4)
Finland	19	(0.8)	33	(1.1)	30	(1.1)	19	(0.9)	17	(1.1)	20	(0.9)	28	(1.0)	28	(1.0)
Germany	23	(0.8)	38	(1.2)	35	(1.1)	19	(1.1)	17	(0.8)	17	(0.9)	25	(0.9)	26	(0.9)
Hungary	22	(1.0)	31	(1.1)	33	(1.3)	24	(1.3)	18	(1.1)	21	(1.1)	28	(1.6)	25	(1.4)
Iceland	25	(1.1)	29	(1.1)	28	(1.2)	23	(1.0)	21	(1.0)	19	(1.0)	26	(1.1)	29	(1.1)
Ireland	23	(1.0)	34	(0.9)	31	(1.0)	22	(1.0)	19	(0.9)	20	(0.9)	27	(1.1)	25	(1.1)
Italy	27	(1.0)	33	(1.1)	33	(1.1)	26	(1.1)	15	(0.8)	18	(1.1)	25	(1.0)	23	(1.1)
Korea	22	(1.0)	24	(1.0)	30	(1.1)	27	(1.0)	23	(1.5)	21	(1.1)	25	(1.5)	28	(1.4)
Luxembourg	24	(1.0)	36	(1.2)	36	(1.3)	18	(1.1)	16	(1.1)	20	(1.2)	25	(1.2)	27	(1.4)
Mexico	25	(1.1)	30	(1.0)	26	(1.3)	22	(1.1)	19	(1.0)	23	(1.3)	30	(1.4)	26	(1.3)
New Zealand	24	(0.9)	35	(1.2)	30	(1.3)	19	(1.0)	20	(1.2)	19	(1.0)	27	(1.2)	27	(1.3)
Norway	23	(1.1)	30	(1.1)	32	(1.4)	20	(0.9)	21	(1.2)	17	(1.0)	24	(1.2)	33	(1.3)
Portugal	27	(1.1)	35	(1.1)	32	(1.1)	22	(1.1)	15	(0.9)	21	(1.2)	26	(1.0)	23	(1.2)
Scotland	23	(1.1)	32	(1.4)	33	(1.3)	21	(1.3)	20	(1.2)	18	(1.2)	25	(1.2)	30	(1.6)
Sweden	23	(1.2)	32	(1.2)	30	(1.0)	20	(1.0)	23	(1.0)	18	(0.9)	24	(1.1)	31	(1.0)
Switzerland	23	(1.1)	41	(1.3)	38	(1.3)	18	(1.0)	18	(1.1)	16	(1.1)	21	(1.0)	25	(1.0)
United States	25	(1.3)	32	(1.6)	27	(1.6)	20	(1.3)	18	(1.2)	22	(1.8)	30	(1.2)	26	(1.7)
OECD average	*24*	*(0.2)*	*33*	*(0.3)*	*32*	*(0.3)*	*21*	*(0.2)*	*19*	*(0.2)*	*19*	*(0.2)*	*25*	*(0.3)*	*27*	*(0.2)*
NON-OECD COUNTRIES																
Brazil	21	(1.2)	33	(1.4)	31	(1.2)	21	(1.1)	18	(1.0)	19	(1.2)	31	(1.2)	28	(1.3)
Latvia	27	(1.2)	35	(1.9)	29	(1.6)	19	(1.1)	15	(0.9)	22	(1.2)	29	(1.4)	25	(1.2)
Liechtenstein	18	(2.8)	39	(4.3)	36	(4.2)	15	(2.9)	23	(3.1)	17	(3.7)	23	(3.3)	29	(3.7)
Russian Federation	23	(1.0)	28	(0.7)	27	(0.9)	20	(0.7)	19	(0.8)	25	(1.0)	31	(1.0)	27	(0.8)
Netherlands[2]	22	(1.4)	38	(1.9)	39	(1.7)	20	(1.5)	20	(1.6)	14	(1.5)	19	(1.3)	27	(1.6)

1. Cluster 1: strongest learners; Cluster 2: stronger learners, weaker in mathematics; Cluster 3: weaker learners, stronger in mathematics; Cluster 4: weakest learners.
2. Response rate is too low to ensure comparability.

Table C4.1
Gender and learner characteristics: Effect sizes

	Memorisation strategies	Control strategies	Elaboration strategies	Effort and persistence	Instrumental motivation	Interest in reading	Interest in mathematics	Preferences for co-operative learning	Preferences for competitive learning	Self-efficacy	Self-concept in reading	Self-concept in mathematics	Academic self-concept
OECD COUNTRIES													
Australia	0.07	0.14	-0.12	0.08	-0.12	0.36	-0.28	0.03	-0.32	-0.22	0.21	-0.29	-0.05
Austria	0.28	0.19	-0.14	0.08	-0.05	0.62	-0.38	0.17	-0.15	-0.32	0.34	-0.30	0.10
Belgium (Fl.)	0.14	0.16	-0.19	0.21	-0.05	0.54	-0.16	0.14	-0.23	-0.24	0.18	-0.27	-0.08
Czech Republic	0.31	0.34	-0.05	0.20	0.12	0.79	-0.26	0.15	-0.01	-0.30	0.37	-0.31	0.05
Denmark	-0.09	0.04	-0.13	0.12	-0.25	0.53	-0.28	-0.02	-0.25	-0.45	0.31	-0.40	-0.16
Finland	0.09	0.12	-0.14	0.25	0.02	0.96	-0.28	0.11	-0.30	-0.34	0.45	-0.36	0.04
Germany	0.28	0.21	-0.08	0.16	0.00	0.60	-0.38	0.10	-0.16	-0.21	0.43	-0.42	0.00
Hungary	0.33	0.27	-0.11	0.17	0.05	0.49	-0.05	0.01	0.02	-0.19	0.33	-0.13	0.08
Iceland	-0.02	0.01	-0.11	0.21	0.01	0.45	-0.02	-0.08	-0.28	-0.26	0.20	-0.19	0.05
Ireland	0.26	0.31	0.05	0.23	-0.08	0.53	-0.13	-0.23	-0.39	-0.17	0.13	-0.11	0.21
Italy	-0.02	0.38	-0.04	0.26	-0.22	0.58	-0.09	-0.27	-0.14	-0.19	0.40	-0.16	0.21
Korea	0.07	0.05	-0.01	-0.03	-0.05	0.02	-0.07	-0.14	-0.12	-0.15	-0.03	-0.16	-0.12
Luxembourg	0.36	0.29	0.06	0.24	0.15	0.43	-0.27	0.19	-0.13	-0.18	0.18	-0.28	0.06
Mexico	-0.03	0.20	0.08	0.20	0.01	0.32	0.02	0.11	-0.13	-0.01	0.25	-0.09	0.06
New Zealand	0.12	0.19	-0.01	0.09	-0.06	0.37	-0.24	0.08	-0.28	-0.19	0.27	-0.26	-0.05
Norway	-0.29	-0.18	-0.21	0.03	-0.09	0.60	-0.38	0.15	-0.34	-0.33	0.37	-0.44	-0.05
Portugal	0.02	0.34	0.03	0.29	0.11	0.80	0.02	0.14	-0.38	-0.14	0.32	-0.16	-0.02
Scotland	0.14	0.22	-0.11	0.14	-0.02	0.43	-0.17	0.05	-0.42	-0.32	0.14	-0.24	-0.03
Sweden	-0.11	-0.02	-0.29	0.02	-0.08	0.47	-0.35	-0.05	-0.27	-0.37	0.37	-0.41	-0.08
Switzerland	0.17	0.24	-0.04	0.16	0.04	0.68	-0.51	0.14	-0.30	-0.22	0.35	-0.55	-0.05
United States	0.17	0.31	0.08	0.31	0.05	0.36	-0.08	0.21	-0.13	-0.06	0.36	-0.13	0.11
OECD average	*0.10*	*0.18*	*-0.06*	*0.16*	*-0.02*	*0.53*	*-0.20*	*0.10*	*-0.21*	*-0.22*	*0.29*	*-0.25*	*0.02*
NON-OECD COUNTRIES													
Brazil	0.10	0.17	0.11	0.19	0.13	0.43	-0.08	0.12	-0.21	-0.09	0.30	-0.21	-0.05
Latvia	0.18	0.25	-0.03	0.15	0.14	0.61	-0.03	0.15	0.11	-0.05	0.51	-0.18	0.11
Liechtenstein	0.18	0.12	-0.21	0.11	-0.08	0.42	-0.71	0.09	-0.36	-0.12	0.37	-0.58	-0.01
Russian Federation	0.20	0.19	-0.09	0.18	0.16	0.41	0.03	0.05	0.10	-0.11	0.48	0.00	0.12
Netherlands[1]	0.03	0.05	-0.19	0.08	-0.17	0.70	-0.48	0.20	-0.34	-0.44	0.26	-0.57	-0.20

1. Response rate is too low to ensure comparability.

Female students have statistically significantly higher scores.

No statistically significant difference between scores of males and females.

Male students have statistically significantly higher scores.

Table C4.2
Socio-economic background[1] and learner characteristics: Effect sizes

	Memorisation strategies	Control strategies	Elaboration strategies	Effort and persistence	Instrumental motivation	Interest in reading	Interest in mathematics	Preferences for co-operative learning	Preferences for competitive learning	Self-efficacy	Self-concept in reading	Self-concept in mathematics	Academic self-concept
Australia	0.11	0.36	0.18	0.27	0.03	0.42	0.14	-0.22	0.31	0.37	0.31	0.20	0.39
Austria	-0.28	0.15	0.14	-0.08	-0.30	0.38	-0.19	-0.11	-0.03	0.29	0.27	0.00	0.23
Belgium (Fl.)	-0.28	0.10	0.03	-0.04	-0.17	0.34	0.18	-0.06	-0.13	0.15	0.06	0.05	0.02
Czech Republic	-0.28	0.34	0.31	0.08	0.05	0.27	0.12	-0.12	0.21	0.34	0.32	0.21	0.31
Denmark	0.10	0.19	0.22	0.25	0.03	0.30	0.18	-0.16	0.15	0.63	0.44	0.41	0.59
Finland	0.07	0.22	0.28	0.26	0.26	0.20	0.33	-0.14	0.26	0.44	0.40	0.49	0.54
Germany	-0.16	0.32	0.38	0.12	-0.10	0.40	-0.01	-0.08	0.04	0.40	0.28	0.06	0.19
Hungary	0.17	0.25	0.18	0.17	-0.05	0.31	0.23	-0.18	0.27	0.39	0.34	0.34	0.33
Iceland	0.17	0.25	0.33	0.16	0.17	0.19	0.34	0.00	0.32	0.60	0.36	0.45	0.51
Ireland	0.01	0.19	0.06	0.07	0.07	0.34	0.02	-0.20	0.29	0.33	0.10	0.07	0.22
Italy	-0.23	0.14	0.13	0.04	-0.09	0.25	-0.04	-0.15	-0.01	0.28	0.27	0.00	0.16
Korea	0.16	0.45	0.51	0.33	0.13	0.30	0.46	0.09	0.40	0.49	0.19	0.47	0.42
Luxembourg	-0.19	0.31	0.06	0.11	0.00	0.13	-0.12	-0.17	-0.03	0.25	0.52	-0.02	0.19
Mexico	0.01	0.30	0.18	-0.03	0.25	-0.06	-0.02	-0.11	0.11	0.37	-0.03	-0.09	0.15
New Zealand	0.11	0.36	0.17	0.11	0.04	0.23	0.03	-0.25	0.25	0.38	0.19	0.35	0.35
Norway	0.11	0.25	0.28	0.29	0.35	0.18	0.35	-0.05	0.44	0.61	0.40	0.54	0.72
Portugal	-0.01	0.44	0.36	0.24	0.14	0.16	0.17	-0.23	-0.07	0.44	0.31	0.27	0.27
Scotland	0.12	0.31	0.14	0.24	0.22	0.42	0.00	-0.15	0.21	0.38	0.26	0.27	0.28
Sweden	0.22	0.41	0.39	0.27	0.22	0.31	0.16	-0.19	0.28	0.60	0.44	0.37	0.51
Switzerland	0.02	0.22	0.21	-0.04	-0.10	0.38	-0.19	-0.19	-0.26	0.28	0.30	-0.16	0.09
United States	-0.03	0.26	0.16	0.20	0.04	0.25	0.05	-0.05	0.29	0.34	0.32	0.25	0.41
OECD average	*-0.01*	*0.26*	*0.22*	*0.14*	*0.06*	*0.26*	*0.10*	*-0.13*	*0.16*	*0.40*	*0.28*	*0.21*	*0.32*
Brazil	0.20	0.29	0.17	0.16	0.15	-0.07	-0.04	-0.08	-0.16	0.22	0.10	0.02	0.06
Latvia	0.09	0.16	0.21	0.10	0.26	0.09	0.12	0.09	0.22	0.34	0.21	0.16	0.30
Liechtenstein	-0.31	-0.25	0.04	0.14	-0.35	0.20	-0.25	-0.21	-0.06	0.10	-0.05	-0.22	-0.15
Russian Federation	0.11	0.28	0.20	0.22	0.29	0.22	0.15	0.06	0.24	0.38	0.36	0.36	0.43
Netherlands[2]	0.03	0.17	0.23	0.09	-0.05	0.24	-0.02	-0.08	0.05	0.24	0.18	0.00	0.04

1. Measured by the International Socio-economic Index of Occupational Status (ISEI) of parents.
2. Response rate is too low to ensure comparability.

Students in top national quarter of socio-economic status have statistically significantly higher scores.

No statistically significant difference between scores of students in top and bottom quarters of socio-economic status.

Students in bottom national quarter of socio-economic status statistically significantly higher scores.

Table C4.3
Immigrant status and learner characteristics: Effect sizes

		Memorisation strategies	Control strategies	Elaboration strategies	Effort and persistence	Instrumental motivation	Interest in reading	Interest in mathematics	Preferences for co-operative learning	Preferences for competitive learning	Self-efficacy	Self-concept in reading	Self-concept in mathematics	Academic self-concept
OECD COUNTRIES	Australia	0.24	0.29	0.32	0.33	0.36	0.11	0.36	-0.13	0.31	0.27	0.07	0.28	0.22
	Austria	0.23	0.05	0.08	0.16	0.15	-0.08	0.25	0.00	0.13	0.01	-0.08	-0.03	0.08
	Belgium (Fl.)	0.26	0.16	0.26	0.20	0.40	-0.08	0.07	-0.06	0.35	0.33	-0.04	-0.05	0.06
	Denmark	0.17	0.28	0.13	0.08	0.09	0.12	0.19	0.10	0.19	0.00	-0.21	0.00	-0.01
	Germany	0.05	-0.06	-0.18	-0.01	0.07	-0.11	0.26	-0.16	-0.02	-0.10	-0.26	0.15	-0.07
	Luxembourg	0.30	-0.11	0.14	-0.09	-0.04	0.02	0.37	0.21	0.20	-0.02	-0.69	0.18	-0.01
	New Zealand	0.21	0.30	0.25	0.26	0.28	0.16	0.54	-0.04	0.43	0.19	-0.20	0.38	0.07
	Norway	0.19	0.32	0.25	0.14	0.11	0.23	0.33	-0.12	0.26	0.14	-0.03	0.07	0.16
	Sweden	0.13	0.17	0.22	0.23	0.16	-0.02	0.41	0.10	0.30	0.18	0.20	0.18	0.26
	Switzerland	0.20	0.04	-0.03	0.06	0.20	-0.16	0.35	0.13	0.31	-0.01	-0.09	0.17	0.04
	United States	0.09	0.11	0.13	0.12	0.27	0.23	0.21	-0.21	0.27	0.13	-0.03	0.10	0.07
	OECD average	*0.23*	*0.17*	*0.15*	*0.08*	*0.16*	*0.03*	*0.32*	*-0.04*	*0.25*	*0.07*	*-0.18*	*0.17*	*0.04*
NON-OECD COUNTRIES	**Latvia**	**0.11**	**0.13**	**0.04**	**0.03**	**0.31**	**-0.13**	**-0.55**	**-0.60**	**-0.23**	**-0.04**	**-0.11**	**-0.20**	**-0.29**
	Liechtenstein	**-0.02**	**-0.10**	**0.08**	**-0.14**	**-0.03**	**-0.01**	**0.50**	**-0.16**	**-0.02**	**-0.25**	**-0.58**	**-0.01**	**-0.08**
	Netherlands[1]	0.31	0.31	0.24	0.40	0.57	0.19	0.20	0.14	0.40	0.21	0.18	0.06	0.23

1. Response rate is too low to ensure comparability.

Immigrant students have statistically significantly higher scores.

No statistically significant difference between scores of immigrant and native students.

Native students have statistically significantly higher scores.

Table C4.4
Performance in reading and learner characteristics: Effect sizes

	Memorisation strategies	Control strategies	Elaboration strategies	Effort and persistence	Instrumental motivation	Interest in reading	Interest in mathematics	Preferences for co-operative learning	Preferences for competitive learning	Self-efficacy	Self-concept in reading	Self-concept in mathematics	Academic self-concept
OECD COUNTRIES													
Australia	0.24	0.62	0.32	0.41	0.14	1.00	0.03	-0.23	0.35	0.56	0.77	0.39	0.84
Austria	-0.36	0.48	0.28	0.08	-0.17	0.97	-0.22	-0.10	0.17	0.52	0.73	0.20	0.67
Belgium (Fl.)	-0.23	0.33	-0.02	0.12	-0.01	0.61	0.01	-0.25	-0.19	0.38	0.42	-0.04	0.30
Czech Republic	-0.36	0.80	0.54	0.19	0.14	1.00	0.05	-0.03	0.35	0.48	0.76	0.38	0.70
Denmark	0.08	0.31	0.30	0.49	0.08	0.87	0.33	-0.37	0.40	0.92	1.02	0.74	1.28
Finland	0.15	0.40	0.42	0.71	0.55	1.19	0.47	-0.13	0.46	0.78	1.06	0.92	1.31
Germany	-0.08	0.59	0.52	0.35	-0.08	0.95	-0.03	-0.06	0.25	0.55	0.58	0.14	0.54
Hungary	0.39	0.43	0.24	0.35	0.07	0.89	0.16	-0.34	0.37	0.36	0.72	0.39	0.55
Iceland	-0.10	0.36	0.36	0.55	0.30	1.01	0.46	-0.12	0.48	0.99	0.88	0.89	1.40
Ireland	0.15	0.56	0.20	0.29	0.17	1.05	0.07	-0.12	0.36	0.61	0.29	0.41	0.78
Italy	-0.42	0.45	0.21	0.21	-0.21	0.67	0.06	-0.07	0.08	0.38	0.69	0.42	0.69
Korea	0.13	0.71	0.86	0.51	0.34	0.79	0.64	0.06	0.66	0.71	0.80	0.49	0.81
Luxemburg	-0.10	0.53	0.27	0.32	0.34	0.59	-0.29	-0.16	-0.07	0.44	0.89	-0.07	0.50
Mexico	0.00	0.66	0.31	0.27	0.48	0.15	0.10	-0.11	0.18	0.56	0.28	0.11	0.43
New Zealand	0.26	0.71	0.18	0.36	0.06	0.90	-0.05	-0.12	0.38	0.54	0.62	0.58	1.00
Norway	-0.15	0.29	0.42	0.66	0.60	1.05	0.33	0.11	0.65	0.97	0.97	0.89	1.47
Portugal	-0.06	0.98	0.59	0.55	0.41	0.71	0.16	-0.09	-0.25	0.69	0.82	0.34	0.72
Scotland	0.07	0.64	0.23	0.41	0.31	1.12	0.14	-0.12	0.32	0.62	0.41	0.68	0.77
Sweden	0.18	0.48	0.33	0.39	0.28	1.01	0.05	-0.37	0.27	0.85	0.94	0.60	1.05
Switzerland	0.05	0.50	0.36	0.21	-0.02	0.92	-0.17	-0.07	-0.13	0.52	0.62	0.02	0.48
United States	0.03	0.55	0.19	0.36	-0.02	0.71	0.09	0.06	0.51	0.69	0.90	0.43	1.06
OECD average	*-0.02*	*0.52*	*0.33*	*0.37*	*0.19*	*0.80*	*0.10*	*-0.09*	*0.23*	*0.61*	*0.69*	*0.37*	*0.74*
NON-OECD COUNTRIES													
Brazil	0.41	0.74	0.53	0.66	0.81	0.20	0.26	-0.12	-0.18	0.66	0.40	0.23	0.26
Latvia	0.15	0.46	0.21	0.22	0.61	0.82	0.22	0.12	0.49	0.50	0.90	0.17	0.68
Liechtenstein	-0.08	0.56	0.37	0.51	0.00	0.87	-0.29	-0.03	-0.08	0.60	0.54	-0.07	0.42
Russian Federation	0.34	0.61	0.28	0.46	0.57	0.61	0.29	-0.02	0.39	0.66	0.74	0.60	0.92
Netherlands[1]	-0.13	0.23	0.06	0.09	-0.22	0.76	-0.20	0.01	-0.09	0.36	0.38	-0.15	0.41

1. Response rate is too low to ensure comparability.

Top quarter of readers has statistically significantly higher scores on the learner characteristics scale than the bottom quarter of readers.

No statistically significant difference between scores on the learner characteristics scale between the top and bottom quarter of readers.

Bottom quarter of readers has statistically significantly higher scores on the learner characteristics scale than the top quarter of readers.

Table C4.5
Difference in the socio-economic background (HISEI[1]) of students

	Mean HISEI of students from lower socio-economic backgrounds		Mean HISEI of students from higher socio-economic backgrounds		Difference
OECD COUNTRIES					
Australia	31.1	(0.2)	73.2	(0.3)	42.1
Austria	32.9	(0.2)	69.1	(0.3)	36.2
Belgium[2]	28.4	(0.1)	71.8	(0.2)	43.4
Czech Republic	31.2	(0.2)	66.1	(0.3)	34.9
Denmark	29.0	(0.2)	71.1	(0.3)	42.1
Finland	29.7	(0.2)	71.8	(0.2)	42.1
Germany	30.0	(0.2)	70.2	(0.2)	40.2
Hungary	30.4	(0.2)	71.5	(0.2)	41.1
Iceland	31.4	(0.2)	73.8	(0.2)	42.4
Ireland	28.5	(0.2)	69.4	(0.2)	40.9
Italy	28.5	(0.1)	68.9	(0.4)	40.4
Korea	26.5	(0.1)	62.9	(0.5)	36.4
Luxembourg	25.1	(0.1)	66.1	(0.4)	41.0
Mexico	24.4	(0.1)	66.5	(0.5)	42.1
New Zealand	30.5	(0.3)	73.6	(0.2)	43.1
Norway	35.6	(0.2)	73.9	(0.2	38.3
Portugal	26.8	(0.2)	65.7	(0.5)	38.9
Sweden	30.4	(0.2)	72.1	(0.2)	41.7
Switzerland	29.3	(0.2)	71.9	(0.3)	42.6
United Kingdom[2]	30.7	(0.2)	71.8	(0.2)	41.1
United States	30.3	(0.2)	72.5	(0.3)	42.2
OECD average	*29.1*	*(0.1)*	*70.3*	*(0.1)*	*41.2*
NON-OECD COUNTRIES					
Brazil	24.6	(0.2)	67.1	(0.4)	42.5
Latvia	27.7	(0.1)	74.1	(0.3)	46.4
Liechtenstein	28.0	(0.6)	68.2	(0.9)	40.2
Russian Federation	30.0	(0.2)	78.9	(0.2)	43.9
Netherlands[3]	29.5	(0.2)	71.3	(0.2)	41.8

1. Measured by the International Socio-Economic Index of Occupational Status of mother or father, whichever is higher.
2. Reported for the whole country.
3. Response rate is too low to ensure comparability.

Table C4.6
Percentage of immigrant students, first generation students and native students

		Immigrant students		First generation students		Native students	
		%	S.E.	%	S.E.	%	S.E.
COUNTRIES INCLUDED IN THE ANALYSIS	Australia	11.9	(1.2)	10.7	(1.1)	77.4	(1.8)
	Austria	5.9	(0.6)	3.7	(0.4)	90.4	(0.9)
	Belgium[1]	3.4	(0.4)	8.6	(0.9)	88.0	(1.1)
	Denmark	3.8	(0.4)	2.4	(0.4)	93.8	(0.6)
	Germany	10.1	(0.6)	5.1	(0.5)	84.8	(0.8)
	Latvia	20.6	(2.4)	1.5	(0.3)	77.9	(2.4)
	Liechtenstein	10.4	(1.6)	10.2	(1.8)	79.4	(2.1)
	Luxembourg	16.4	(0.6)	17.8	(0.7)	65.8	(0.7)
	New Zealand	13.2	(0.8)	6.4	(0.5)	80.4	(1.1)
	Norway	3.1	(0.3)	1.5	(0.2)	95.4	(0.4)
	Sweden	5.9	(0.6)	4.7	(0.6)	89.5	(0.9)
	Switzerland	11.4	(0.7)	9.3	(0.6)	79.3	(0.9)
	United States	6.1	(0.9)	7.4	(1.4)	86.4	(2.1)
	OECD average	*5.2*	*(0.1)*	*4.5*	*(0.1)*	*90.4*	*(0.2)*
	Netherlands[2]	4.5	(0.8)	7.4	(1.2)	88.1	(1.8)
COUNTRIES NOT INCLUDED IN THE ANALYSIS	Brazil	0.1	(0.1)	0.3	(0.1)	99.6	(0.1)
	Czech Republic	0.5	(0.1)	0.6	(0.1)	98.9	(0.2)
	Finland	1.0	(0.2)	0.2	(0.1)	98.7	(0.2)
	Hungary	1.6	(0.2)	0.1	(0)	98.3	(0.2)
	Iceland	0.6	(0.1)	0.2	(0.1)	99.2	(0.2)
	Ireland	1.4	(0.3)	0.9	(0.2)	97.7	(0.3)
	Italy	0.8	(0.2)	0.2	(0.1)	99.1	(0.2)
	Mexico	2.5	(0.3)	1.1	(0.2)	96.4	(0.4)
	Portugal	1.4	(0.2)	1.8	(0.2)	96.9	(0.3)
	Russian Federation	2.8	(0.4)	1.8	(0.3)	95.4	(0.6)
	United Kingdom	2.6	(0.4)	7.0	(0.9)	90.4	(1.2)

1. Reported for the whole country.
2. Response rate is too low to ensure comparability.

Table C4.7
Percentage of students who speak the language of assessment or other languages by immigrant status

	All students				Native students				Immigrant students			
	Language of assessment		Other language		Language of assessment		Other language		Language of assessment		Other language	
	%	S.E.	%	S.E.	%	S.E.	%	S.E.	%	S.E.	%	S.E.
Australia	83	(1.6)	17	(1.6)	95	(0.6)	5	(0.6)	36	(4.7)	64	(4.7)
Austria	93	(0.7)	7	(0.7)	99	(0.2)	1	(0.2)	21	(3.8)	79	(3.8)
Belgium [1]	95	(0.6)	5	(0.6)	99	(0.2)	1	(0.2)	75	(3.4)	25	(3.4)
Denmark	93	(0.4)	7	(0.4)	98	(0.3)	2	(0.3)	24	(3.8)	76	(3.8)
Germany	92	(0.8)	8	(0.8)	99	(0.1)	1	(0.1)	32	(3.4)	68	(3.4)
Luxembourg	82	(0.7)	18	(0.7)	99	(0.2)	1	(0.2)	36	(2.1)	64	(2.1)
New Zealand	90	(0.6)	10	(0.6)	99	(0.1)	1	(0.1)	44	(2.6)	56	(2.6)
Norway	95	(0.4)	5	(0.4)	98	(0.2)	2	(0.2)	15	(4.2)	85	(4.2)
Sweden	93	(0.6)	7	(0.6)	99	(0.1)	1	(0.1)	18	(2.5)	82	(2.5)
Switzerland	86	(0.6)	14	(0.6)	97	(0.3)	3	(0.3)	27	(2.1)	73	(2.1)
United States	89	(2.4)	11	(2.4)	97	(0.9)	3	(0.9)	29	(4.1)	71	(4.1)
OECD average	*90*	*(0.3)*	*10*	*(0.3)*	*98*	*(0.2)*	*2*	*(0.2)*	*34*	*(1.1)*	*66*	*(1.1)*
Liechtenstein	79	(2.2)	21	(2.2)	88	(2.2)	12	(2.2)	28	(8.0)	72	(8.0)
Netherlands [2]	95	(1.1)	5	(1.1)	100	(0.2)	0	(0.2)	4	(6.9)	60	(6.9)

1. Reported for the whole country.
2. Response rate is too low to ensure comparability.

Table C4.8a
Distribution of top and bottom quarters of readers across the five reading literacy proficiency levels

	Reader group[1]	Percentage of students at each proficiency level					
		Below Level 1	Level 1	Level 2	Level 3	Level 4	Level 5
OECD COUNTRIES Australia	Top quarter				1.6	35.7	62.7
	Bottom quarter	13.3	36.2	45.6	4.9		
Austria	Top quarter				7.4	58.5	34.1
	Bottom quarter	17.7	39.6	40.3	2.4		
Belgium[2]	Top quarter			0.1	4.0	50.5	45.5
	Bottom quarter	30.7	42.5	25.7	1.1		
Czech Republic	Top quarter			0.2	14.3	57.9	27.6
	Bottom quarter	24.3	42.4	32.4	0.9		
Denmark	Top quarter			0.1	10.1	57.9	31.9
	Bottom quarter	23.5	44.9	30.6	0.9		
Finland	Top quarter				1.0	34.9	64.1
	Bottom quarter	6.9	20.8	49.6	22.3	0.4	
Germany	Top quarter			0.1	10.9	54.2	34.9
	Bottom quarter	39.7	43.6	16.5	0.3	0.1	
Hungary	Top quarter		0.3	1.1	19.1	59.3	20.2
	Bottom quarter	27.5	51.7	20.0	0.8		
Iceland	Top quarter				8.4	56.7	34.9
	Bottom quarter	15.8	40.4	40.5	3.3		
Ireland	Top quarter				3.0	44.3	52.7
	Bottom quarter	12.3	31.3	47.6	8.7	0.1	
Italy	Top quarter			0.2	17.7	60.8	21.4
	Bottom quarter	21.5	48.9	28.9	0.7		
Korea	Top quarter				10.2	67.6	22.2
	Bottom quarter	3.6	19.2	57.3	19.8	0.3	
Luxembourg	Top quarter		0.6	3.6	46.1	43.0	6.6
	Bottom quarter	53.3	41.8	4.8	0.1		
Mexico	Top quarter		0.2	15.0	57.5	23.9	3.4
	Bottom quarter	58.9	39.4	1.6			
New Zealand	Top quarter				0.9	32.0	67.1
	Bottom quarter	19.3	35.3	41.0	4.3		
Norway	Top quarter				4.8	51.5	43.6
	Bottom quarter	25.2	42.6	30.8	1.3		
Portugal	Top quarter			0.2	25.6	57.3	16.9
	Bottom quarter	38.3	49.5	12.0	0.2		
Sweden	Top quarter			0.1	4.9	52.1	42.9
	Bottom quarter	13.3	36.6	46.3	3.8		
Switzerland	Top quarter			0.1	9.6	54.1	36.3
	Bottom quarter	28.2	48.3	22.9	0.6		
United Kingdom[2]	Top quarter				2.4	38.1	59.5
	Bottom quarter	14.4	36.2	44.5	4.8	0.1	
United States	Top quarter			0.1	5.5	47.4	47.1
	Bottom quarter	25.7	43.4	29.9	1.0	0.2	
OECD average	*Top quarter*			*0.9*	*12.1*	*49.2*	*37.7*
	Bottom quarter	*23.7*	*39.3*	*32.7*	*4.3*		
NON-OECD COUNTRIES Brazil	Top quarter		1.3	35.5	48.8	12.3	2.2
	Bottom quarter	77.3	22.3	0.4			
Latvia	Top quarter			0.7	33.0	49.7	16.6
	Bottom quarter	48.0	46.2	5.8			
Liechtenstein	Top quarter			1.2	19.0	59.8	20.0
	Bottom quarter	30.6	51.0	18.4			
Russian Federation	Top quarter			1.3	36.2	49.8	12.8
	Bottom quarter	35.5	53.0	11.4	0.1		

1. Students in the top and bottom national quarters based on their reading literacy performance.
2. Reported for the whole country.

Table C4.8b
**Difference between top and bottom quarters of readers on
the combined reading literacy scale**

	Difference[1] between readers in top and bottom quaters
OECD COUNTRIES	
Australia	259
Austria	235
Belgium [2]	267
Czech Republic	237
Denmark	244
Finland	222
Germany	263
Hungary	235
Iceland	232
Ireland	234
Italy	228
Korea	181
Luxembourg	262
Mexico	227
New Zealand	269
Norway	258
Portugal	243
Sweden	234
Switzerland	251
United Kingdom	254
United States	258
OECD average	*242*
NON-OECD COUNTRIES	
Brazil	256
Latvia	256
Liechtenstein	235
Russian Federation	233

1. Differences of average scores on the combined reading literacy scale.
2. Reported for the whole country.

STANDARD ERRORS, SIGNIFICANCE TESTS, EFFECT SIZES AND STRUCTURAL EQUATION MODELS

The statistics in this report represent *estimates* of national performance based on samples of students rather than values that could be calculated if every student in every country had answered every question. Consequently, it is important to have measures of the degree of uncertainty of the estimates. In PISA 2000, each estimate has an associated degree of uncertainty, which is expressed through a *standard error*. The use of *confidence intervals* provides a way to make inferences about the population means and proportions in a manner that reflects the uncertainty associated with the sample estimates. From an observed sample statistic it can, under the assumption of a normal distribution, be inferred that the corresponding population result would lie within the confidence interval in 95 out of 100 replications of the measurement on different samples drawn from the same population.

In many cases, readers are primarily interested in whether a given value in a particular country is different from a second value in the same or another country, *e.g.*, whether females in a country perform better than males in the same country. In the tables and charts used in this report, differences are labelled as *statistically significant* when a difference of that size, or larger, would be observed less than 5 per cent of the time, if there was actually no difference in corresponding population values. Similarly, the risk of reporting as significant if there is, in fact, no correlation between two measures is contained at 5 per cent.

For all other tables and charts readers should note that, if there were no real differences on a given measure, then the *multiple comparison* in conjunction with a 5 per cent significance level, would erroneously identify differences on 0.05 times the number of comparisons made. For example, even though the significance tests applied in PISA for identifying gender differences ensure that, for each country, the likelihood of identifying a gender difference erroneously is less than 5 per cent, a comparison showing differences for 20 countries would, on average, identify 1.4 cases (0.05 times 27) with significant gender differences, even if there were no real gender differences in any of the countries. The same applies for other statistics for which significance tests have been undertaken in this publication, such as correlations and regression coefficients.

In Chapter 3, the differences between subgroups of students were displayed as effect sizes. To understand what an effect size is, it is important to introduce a broader concept: comparison in terms of a standard. Many statistical formulas are based on standardised comparisons. For example, the simplest way to compare the average income in France and Mexico is to do so in terms of euros or US dollars. By the same token, a t-test is a mean comparison in terms of the standard deviation. Effect size can thus be conceptualised as a standardised difference. In its simplest form, effect size, which is denoted by the symbol "d", is the mean difference between groups in standard score form, *i.e.*, the ratio of the difference between the means to the standard deviation Accordingly, throughout this report, effect sizes were calculated as: mean of group 1 minus mean of group 2 divided by the pooled standard deviation of both groups. The conventional values for effect size are: small d = 0.20; medium d = 0.50; large d = 0.80.

In Chapter 2, structural equation models are used. This statistical procedure allows for goodness of fit tests as well as simultaneous estimations of the specific, combined, mediated and direct effects of the factors outlined in the model from a country-comparative perspective. As is the case in all multiple regression analyses, effects of the standardised regression coefficients from the multiple regression were calculated simultaneously, and thus appear smaller than the bivariate effects. The simultaneously estimated effects of the structural equation model show the effect of each factor when the other factors are held constant. By analysing the specific and combined effects of the predictor variables of the model, it is possible to determine the relative importance of each factor.

The multi-group model was computed with a number of equality constraints, assuming invariant reliability coefficients across countries as well as invariant structural patterns. The goodness of fit statistics for the model indicate an acceptable model fit across countries (chi^2 = 31181; chi^2 /df = 9.59 df = 3251; RMSEA = 0.008, CFI = 0.99, TLI = 0.99).

Annex

E

THE DEVELOPMENT OF THE PISA THEMATIC REPORT – A COLLABORATIVE EFFORT

Introduction

PISA is a collaborative effort, bringing together scientific expertise from the participating countries, steered jointly by their governments on the basis of shared, policy-driven interests.

A Board of Participating Countries on which each country is represented determines, in the context of OECD objectives, the policy priorities for PISA and oversees adherence to these priorities during the implementation of the programme. This includes the setting of priorities for the development of indicators, for the establishment of the assessment instruments and for the reporting of the results.

Experts from participating countries also serve on working groups that are charged with linking policy objectives with the best internationally available technical expertise. By participating in these expert groups, countries ensure that: the instruments are internationally valid and take into account the cultural and educational contexts in OECD Member countries; the assessment materials have strong measurement properties; and the instruments place an emphasis on authenticity and educational validity.

Through National Project Managers, participating countries implement PISA at the national level subject to the agreed administration procedures. National Project Managers play a vital role in ensuring that the implementation of the survey is of high quality, and verify and evaluate the survey results, analyses, reports and publications.

The design and implementation of the surveys, within the framework established by the Board of Participating Countries, is the responsibility of the PISA Consortium, referred to as the PISA Consortium, led by the Australian Council for Educational Research (ACER). Other partners in this Consortium include the Netherlands National Institute for Educational Measurement (Citogroep), The National Institute for Educational Research in Japan (NIER), the Educational Testing Service in the United States (ETS), and WESTAT in the United States.

The OECD Secretariat has overall managerial responsibility for the programme, monitors its implementation on a day-to-day basis, acts as the secretariat for the Board of Participating Countries, builds consensus among countries and serves as the interlocutor between the Board of Participating Countries and the international consortium charged with the implementation of the activities. The OECD Secretariat also produces the indicators and analyses and prepares the international reports and publications in co-operation with the PISA Consortium and in close consultation with Member countries both at the policy level (Board of Participating Countries) and at the level of implementation (National Project Managers).

The following lists the members of the various PISA bodies and the individual experts and consultants who have contributed to PISA.

Members of the PISA 2000 Board of Participating Countries

Chair: Eugene Owen

Australia: Wendy Whitham
Austria: Friedrich Plank
Belgium: Dominique Barthélémy, Christiane Blondin, Dominique Lafontaine, Liselotte van de Perre
Brazil: Maria Helena Guimarães de Castro
Canada: Satya Brink, Patrick Bussière, Dianne Pennock
Czech Republic: Jan Koucky, Jana Strakova
Denmark: Birgitte Bovin
Finland: Ritva Jakku-Sihvonen
France: Gérard Bonnet
Germany: Jochen Schweitzer, Helga Hinke, Gudrun Stoltenberg
Greece: Vassilis Koulaidis
Hungary: Péter Vári
Iceland: Einar Gudmundsson
Ireland: Gerry Shiel
Italy: Chiara Croce, Elisabetta Midena, Benedetto Vertecchi
Japan: Ryo Watanabe
Korea: Kooghyang Ro
Latvia: Andris Kangro
Luxembourg: Jean-Paul Reeff
Mexico: Fernando Córdova Calderón
Netherlands: Arnold Spee
New Zealand: Lynne Whitney
Norway: Alette Schreiner
Poland: Kazimierz Korab
Portugal: Glória Ramalho
Russian Federation: Galina Kovalyova
Spain: Guillermo Gil
Sweden: Anders Auer, Birgitta Fredander, Anita Wester
Switzerland: Heinz Gilomen
United Kingdom: Lorna Bertrand, Brian Semple
United States: Mariann Lemke

PISA 2000 National Project Managers

Australia: Jan Lokan
Austria: Günter Haider
Belgium: Dominique Lafontaine, Luc van de Poele

Brazil: Tereza Cristina Cotta, Maria Lucia Guardia, Maria Inês Pestana

Canada: Marc Lachance, Dianne Pennock
Czech Republic: Jana Straková
Denmark: Vita Bering Pruzan
Finland: Jouni Välijärvi
France: Jean-Pierre Jeantheau
Germany: Juergen Baumert, Petra Stanat
Greece: Katerina Kassotakis
Hungary: Péter Vári
Iceland: Julius Bjornsson, Ragna Benedikta Garðarsdóttir
Ireland: Judith Cosgrove
Italy: Emma Nardi
Japan: Ryo Watanabe
Korea: Kooghyang Ro
Latvia: Andris Kangro
Luxembourg: Iris Blanke, Jean-Paul Reeff
Mexico: Fernando Córdova Calderón
Netherlands: Johan Wijnstra
New Zealand: Steve May
Norway: Svein Lie
Poland: Michal Federowicz
Portugal: Glória Ramalho
Russian Federation: Galina Kovalyova
Spain: Guillermo Gil
Sweden: Bengt-Olov Molander, Astrid Pettersson, Karin Taube
Switzerland: Huguette McCluskey
United Kingdom: Baljit Gill, Graham Thorpe
United States: Ghedam Bairu, Marilyn Binkley

OECD Secretariat

Andreas Schleicher (overall co-ordination of PISA and Member country relations)
Kooghyang Ro (thematic analyses)
Claudia Tamassia (project management)
Eric Charbonnier (statistical support)
Hannah Cocks (statistical support)
Juliet Evans (administrative support)

PISA Expert groups

Reading Functional Expert Group

Irwin Kirsch (Chair) (Educational Testing Service, United States)
Marilyn Binkley (National Center for Educational Statistics, United States)

Alan Davies (University of Edinburgh, United Kingdom)
Stan Jones (Statistics Canada, Canada)
John de Jong (Language Testing Services, The Netherlands)
Dominique Lafontaine (Université de Liège, Sart Tilman, Belgium)
Pirjo Linnakylä (University of Jyväskylä, Finland)
Martine Rémond (Institut National de Recherche Pédagogique, France)
Wolfgang Schneider (University of Würzburg, Germany)
Ryo Watanabe (National Institute for Educational Research, Japan)

PISA Technical Advisory Group

Ray Adams (ACER, Australia)
Pierre Foy (Statistics Canada, Canada)
Aletta Grisay (Belgium)
Larry Hedges (The University of Chicago, United States)
Eugene Johnson (American Institutes for Research, United States)
John de Jong (Language Testing Services, The Netherlands)
Geoff Masters (ACER, Australia)
Keith Rust (WESTAT, United States)
Norman Verhelst (Cito group, The Netherlands)
J. Douglas Willms (University of New Brunswick, Canada)

PISA Consortium

Australian Council for Educational Research

Ray Adams (Project Director of the PISA Consortium)
Alla Berezner (data processing, data analysis)
Claus Carstensen (data analysis)
Lynne Darkin (reading test development)
Brian Doig (mathematics test development)
Adrian Harvey-Beavis (quality monitoring, questionnaire development)
Kathryn Hill (reading test development)

John Lindsey (mathematics test development)
Jan Lokan (quality monitoring, field procedures development)
Le Tu Luc (data processing)
Greg Macaskill (data processing)
Joy McQueen (reading test development and reporting)
Gary Marks (questionnaire development)
Juliette Mendelovits (reading test development and reporting)
Christian Monseur (Director of the PISA Consortium for data processing, data analysis, quality monitoring)
Gayl O'Connor (science test development)
Alla Routitsky (data processing)
Wolfram Schulz (data analysis)
Ross Turner (test analysis and reporting co-ordination)
Nikolai Volodin (data processing)
Craig Williams (data processing, data analysis)
Margaret Wu (Deputy Project Director of the PISA Consortium)

Westat

Nancy Caldwell (Director of the PISA Consortium for field operations and quality monitoring)
Ming Chen (sampling and weighting)
Fran Cohen (sampling and weighting)
Susan Fuss (sampling and weighting)
Brice Hart (sampling and weighting)
Sharon Hirabayashi (sampling and weighting)
Sheila Krawchuk (sampling and weighting)
Dward Moore (field operations and quality monitoring)
Phu Nguyen (sampling and weighting)
Monika Peters (field operations and quality monitoring)
Merl Robinson (field operations and quality monitoring)
Keith Rust (Director of the PISA Consortium for sampling and weighting)
Leslie Wallace (sampling and weighting)
Dianne Walsh (field operations and quality monitoring)
Trevor Williams (questionnaire development)

Citogroep

Steven Bakker (science test development)
Bart Bossers (reading test development)
Truus Decker (mathematics test development)
Erna van Hest (reading test development and quality monitoring)
Kees Lagerwaard (mathematics test development)

Gerben van Lent (mathematics test development)
Ico de Roo (science test development)
Maria van Toor (office support and quality monitoring)
Norman Verhelst (technical advice, data analysis)

Educational Testing Service

Irwin Kirsch (reading test development)

Other experts

Cordula Artelt (questionnaire development)
Monique Boekaerts (manuscript review)
Marc Demeuse (quality monitoring)
Harry Ganzeboom (questionnaire development)
Aletta Grisay (technical advice, data analysis,
translation, questionnaire development)
Donald Hirsch (editorial review)
Harry O'Neil (manuscript review)
Jules Peschar (questionnaire development)
Luc Van de Poele (manuscript review)
Erich Ramseier (questionnaire development)
Gundel Schümer (questionnaire development)
Marie-Andrée Somers (data analysis and reporting)
Rich Tobin (questionnaire development and reporting)
J. Douglas Willms (questionnaire development, data
analysis and reporting)

OECD PUBLICATIONS, 2, rue André-Pascal, 75775 PARIS CEDEX 16
PRINTED IN FRANCE
(96 2003 10 1 P) ISBN 92-64-10390-2 – No. 53185 2003